ESCAPE
VELOCITY

ESCAPE
VELOCITY

*Free Your Company's Future
from the Pull of the Past*

GEOFFREY A. MOORE

HARPER
An Imprint of HarperCollins*Publishers*
www.harpercollins.com

HarperCollins books may be purchased for educational, business, or sales promotional use. For information, please write: Special Markets Department, HarperCollins Publishers, 10 East 53rd Street, New York, NY 10022.

FIRST EDITION

Library of Congress Cataloging-in-Publication Data has been applied for.

ISBN: 978-0-06-204089-3

12 13 14 15   OV/RRD   10 9 8 7 6 5 4 3 2

To Pat Granger,

who manages my context so that I may focus on core

and who has become a good friend and trusted adviser

CONTENTS

Acknowledgments

The material in this book is the culmination of a ten-year journey undertaken by my colleagues and me at TCG Advisors to address the challenges faced by incumbent franchises in a high-tech sector characterized by the frequent introduction of disruptive technologies and discontinuous innovations. The founding members of the group, including Todd Hewlin, Lo-Ping Yeh, and Philip Lay, have had the deepest impact, not only on the models and frameworks I describe, but also on my understanding of business in general. In addition, everyone who has participated in our work along the way has left some mark on it, and thanks and acknowledgment in particular need to go to Brett Bonthron, Rick Chavez, John Metcalfe, Tom Kosnik, John Hamm, and Francois Joanette. And then there is the extended "chasm community," which has also weighed in from time to time, including Mark Cavender and Michael Eckhardt from Chasm Institute, and Paul Wiefels, Tom Kippola, and Rene White from the Chasm Group. And finally there are my colleagues at MDV, where

I am a venture partner, in particular those focused on the enterprise IT space—Jon Feiber, Nancy Schoendorf, Bill Ericson, Dave Feinleib, Bryan Stolle, Katherine Barr, Sven Strohband, and Jim Smith—who have further shaped my thinking about the dynamics of high-tech markets.

On the industry side, I would like to thank a number of executives who took the time to brief me about issues specific to their companies and expertise. Without examples that they shared and I have passed along, these models would be dry fare indeed. So thanks in particular to Chris Schoettle, Bob Beauchamp, Raj Nathan, John Chen, Malcolm Frank, Lanham Napier, Todd Bradley, Carl Bass, Roy Vallee, Aart de Geus, Ginny Lee, and Marc Benioff for being so generous with their time. More generally, there are a handful of associates in business who have always proved to be superb sounding boards for new ideas, and in this category I'd like to acknowledge Tim Brown, David Kenny, Marty Coyne, Peter Schireson, Rebecca Jacoby, Paul Saffo, Ron Ricci, Sheldon Laube, Thornton May, Sanjay Vaswani, John Bruno, and Rob Tarkoff.

Finally, on the book end of things, this is yet another way station on my lifelong journey with Jim Levine, my literary agent, who has been an expert guide and thoughtful collaborator in each of these projects, and a wonderful friend to boot. And thanks to Hollis Heimbouch, my editor at Harper-Collins, who along with Jim has helped me grope through the transition from "tree book to e-book," balancing the possible with the probable, and keeping a good spirit at all times. And a future vote of thanks to Pat Granger, my longtime assistant, to whom this book is dedicated, and Nanette Vidan-Peled, both of whom will bear much of the burden in coordinating the launch and promotion efforts to come.

And that brings me to my final support group, the one that

is always there, which at its largest is my extended family and friends; closer in, my children and the wonderful people in their lives, who collectively are the loves of my life; and at the very center of everything, Marie. Writing is a journey that takes you away from the present moment, and living with someone who is both present and not present is deeply demanding. To find Marie there every time I come up for air is both miraculous and profoundly restorative, and without her gifts to me, I would have nothing to give to others.

Introduction

This is a book about freeing your company's future from the pull of the past, but we should ask ourselves right from the start, why should one believe it is in need of liberation? What's the matter with the status quo? Why isn't "Steady as she goes" the mantra of choice, or perhaps "Stay the course"? What change is so dramatic that it calls into question the working assumptions that have sustained successful business performance for the past half century? In a word: *globalization*.

For all my life enterprises hosted in the United States, Western Europe, and Japan have had "home field advantage" in the great growth markets of the twentieth century, with privileged access in particular to the American consumer economy. This is our proud past, and its pull is palpable. In the twenty-first century, however, we can already see that these advantages no longer obtain. The American consumer is as readily accessed from Singapore as Seattle, and the great growth market opportunities will come from the developing, not the developed, economies. Of the next 1.3 billion people to be added to the world population, only 90 million are expected to come from developed-economy countries. This means the current set of global enterprise leaders will have to develop new skills for playing "away games" or see their power marginalized.

At the same time, the first generation of successful enterprises coming out of the developing world also need to reorient themselves to their future, leaving behind a past in which their growth came primarily from penetrating mature markets with lower-cost offers. As their standards of living rise, their cost advantages decline, and playing a game where partners and customers lead and they follow will no longer serve. They themselves must take the lead or again be content to see their power marginalized. One way or another, for everyone involved, globalization means a whole new ball game.

And that means back to the drawing board for vision, strategy, and execution. What, to begin with, do we think this new world will actually want from developed-economy companies? What will it want from IBM? Apple? Google? Microsoft? HP? Dell? More of the same? Well, yes, to some extent—but what else? And what else will it want from *your* company?

Posing that question unlocks a whole storehouse of questions to follow. Which markets will create your best returns, and how will you realign your management and resources to capitalize on them? Who will design your next generation of offers, and for whom will they be designed? Who are becoming your new reference competitors, and how do you stack up against the norms they are setting? On what basis will you be able to differentiate against these competitors sustainably?

And how will your legacy business models stand up in an increasingly digitized, globalized, and virtualized economy? These are vexing questions indeed.

Now, to be sure, the forces we are invoking will take time to unfold. The sky is not falling—yet. There is still plenty of opportunity to read and react, to listen and evolve. If you can make reasonable and steady progress toward staking out positions in next-generation markets, while at the same time leveraging your current positions in current markets, you can be optimistic about your chances. Or can you?

What if there is some hidden force that is working against your best efforts? What if this force is operating inside your own company, with the full support of your executive team, your board of directors, your investors, and indeed yourself? What if this force is able to mysteriously redirect resource allocation so that it never quite gets deployed against the new agendas?

That force, I submit, is the pull of the past, most concretely embodied in your prior year's operating plan. That plan exerts a gravitational force that pulls inexorably at any investments that seek to depart from its inertial path. The larger and more successful the enterprise, the greater the inertial mass, the harder it is to alter course and speed.

This observation may seem commonplace, so let us just take a minute to call to mind how deep these ruts can run.

You are on an annual calendar, and strategic planning begins, say, sometime in Q3 and comes to a close at the end of Q4. How does the process begin? Typically with the CFO circulating last year's operating plan as a benchmark for setting next year's resource allocation and performance goals. ("Just take your fourth-quarter numbers and multiply them by four for a start.") By the way, this is a perfectly acceptable procedure for mature markets with cyclical growth patterns where market shares shift by a small percentage in any given year.

What happens next? The executive staff asks all the participating units to draft a bottoms-up plan for next year while, in tandem, it develops a top-down set of goals and benchmarks. These two efforts converge to shake hands early in the fourth quarter, only to confirm that their positions are so far apart they can barely see each other to wave across the table. From this inauspicious beginning, an extended exercise in stretching and cutting, putting and taking ensues, which takes on the air of something between a late-night poker game and a ritual fire dance. You might call it the ultimate zero-sum game except that it really pursues a minus-sum target, a do-more-with-less result. In any event, it is conducted with all the goodwill and trustworthiness of a used-car sale negotiation, perhaps its greatest virtue being that it makes executives anxious to get back into execution mode.

But again, let me be clear: this is standard operating procedure for squeezing operational gains from mature markets, and to the degree that your enterprise is an established player in such venues, there is nothing inherently wrong with it. OK, it could be done with better grace and less waste of energy, but it does not result, in and of itself, in bad economic results. *Until you expose the enterprise to secular market change.*

Secular growth, in this context, means a "not to be repeated" expansion of the market that occurs whenever a new category or a new class of customers is brought on board. It stands in contrast to *cyclical growth*, which refers to the ongoing returns from an established market, one in which the customers and the category remain the same and power shuttles here and there among various vendors and their latest offers. The key point here is, you can make a mistake with cyclical growth and still have plenty of chances to get yourself back in the game. That is not the case, however, with secular change. Whiff here, and you miss out on a massive growth opportunity that will never pass your way again. In short, missing out on secular growth is a disaster.

But that is precisely what you are about to do. All the resource decision making you and your colleagues are engaging in, after all, is internally focused. It gets resolved not in relation to market opportunity but rather in relation to other players on the same team—I got the head count or you did, and whichever one of us it was, we sure as heck aren't giving it back. Which means when it comes to strategy dialogues, we have to justify the resources we have managed to secure *no matter what*. So we tell strategy stories that have all the authenticity of political advertisements and that collectively add up to a vision so self-centered and self-serving as to be incommunicable outside our immediate ranks. Meanwhile, the entire world is yelling at us that a train is coming, which doesn't help, because we *know* a train is coming, but we are locked into relationships that do not allow any of us to move off the track. In short, we are not stupid, and we are not unaware, we are just well and truly stuck.

But the world outside us is not stuck. It is changing, and the fact that the pace of change is measured no longer reassures, now that we find ourselves sinking deeper and deeper into a fixed legacy position. It is now that we really appreciate the power of the force field around us. We begin to get an inkling that what happened at Burroughs and Sperry Univac and Honeywell and Control Data, what happened at Digital Equipment Company and Wang and Data General and Prime, what happened at Kodak and Polaroid, at Lucent and Nortel, at Compaq and Gateway, what happened at Lotus and Ashton-Tate and

Borland and Novell, what happened at General Motors and Ford and Chrysler, what happened at Eastern Airlines and Western Airlines and Northwest Airlines, what happened at *Businessweek* and *Newsweek* and the *Chicago Tribune*, what happened at Tower Records and Borders, what happened at Motorola and Nokia, what happened at Pacific Bell and Quest and America West and Bell South—what happened at all these companies might just be happening to us.

Well, perhaps it is, but let us be clear: *It does not have to be that way.* There is another path, one that can achieve the escape velocity required to engineer a genuine change in course. This path accommodates both the sustaining demands of cyclical market positions and the disruptive ones of new secular change. Like the one we are currently bound to, it ends with an annual operating plan and a resource negotiation that can have zero-sum or even minus-sum characteristics (although secular growth gives you a lot more leeway to play non-zero-sum games). But it does not start there.

Instead it begins with a highly structured set of dialogues around vision, strategy, and execution that tee up future opportunities and risks in a way that allows them to compete more effectively for resources against our existing franchises. The dialogue process will differ in details from firm to firm but overall will look something like the following:

1. Once a year, at the beginning of the strategic planning process, before circulating last year's plan, before financial goal setting of any kind, you and your colleagues commit to reimagine your enterprise from the outside in. Specifically, you agree to temporarily let go of your inside-out perspective and ask the question we began this introduction with: *What does the world*

really want from us? In other words, what opportunities unfold if you put yourself in service to and take your direction from the people in the world you most want to succeed and who most want you to succeed?

2. Keeping this question in mind and leveraging the framing model of this book, which we call the Hierarchy of Powers, you organize and shape your approach to the planning effort for next year with three goals foremost:

   a. Articulate a compelling vision of the future that others will want to support,

   b. Set a strategy consistent with your vision that positions you as the leader in the markets you want to serve, and

   c. Resource your execution so that it can both accomplish your highest aspirations *and* generate superior economic returns.

To address the first of these goals, the dialogue will use the frameworks around category power, company power, and market power to develop a common vision as to what is happening in the world and how it relates to your business.

To address the second, the focus will step down a level and use the frameworks around company power, market power, and offer power to forge a strategy for sustainable competitive advantage in the markets you have targeted, relative to the companies that also seek to serve those markets.

And to address the third goal, the conversation will step down another level to get to the very base of the model and use the frameworks around market power, offer power, and execution power to construct an operating plan that dramatically skews your resource allocation toward escape velocity initiatives such that your direct competitors either cannot or will not match your commitments.

As you can see from this final step, the resource allocation outcome from this process is categorically different from the one that results from staying within the gravitational field of last year's operating plan. This is not about adding 10 percent or giving back 10 percent on a unit-by-unit basis. You are not trying to maximize your power internally relative to each other. Instead this is all about maximizing your enterprise's ability to create unmatchable power in the world. You are not dividing up a check at a restaurant. You are setting up base camp to climb K2. Or, to leave metaphors behind for a moment, you are doing everything you can to give vision and strategy a chance to make their case before you dive into the zero-sum exercise of resource allocation.

During the past two decades, my colleagues and I have seen this process succeed firsthand at Cisco and Sybase, at Agilent and Cognizant, at Akamai and BEA, at Amdocs and Documentum, at Lawson and Activant, at SAP and BMC, at Agile and PeopleSoft, at Autodesk and Synopsys, at Rackspace and Adobe, at Symbol and Qualcomm, not to mention dozens of Silicon Valley–funded start-ups. Over and over again, executive teams have used these frameworks to align around a common vision that truly means something to people other than themselves, to commit to a strategy that capitalizes on the opportunities unveiled by that vision, and to allocate resources in strikingly asymmetrical ways to create customer success and drive competition from the field.

Now, as you no doubt have noticed, every one of the companies cited above is in high tech, and not accidentally so. This sector has been the exclusive focus of our consulting practice, both at the Chasm Group during the 1990s and at TCG Advisors in the past decade. That focus has allowed us to separate ourselves from our competitive set and compete effectively against enterprises with orders of magnitude larger and more experienced than us. It has also resulted in intimate discussions with the top executives in each of the firms cited above. There is no form of research that can approximate the learning and perspective gained from such engagements.

One consequence of this experience base, however, is that this book clearly does have a high-tech bias, and to the degree your enterprise operates under different norms, you'll have to make allowances (or just chuck the book aside and move on to a more profitable activity). But more and more industries are becoming drawn into the high-tech sector's disruptive field. First it was telecommunications and financial services, along with defense and aerospace. Then the Internet arrived to disrupt retail commerce, media, music, entertainment, and news. Health care is now being touched, and one can only hope education is not far behind. Energy companies are deploying smart grids, automotive enterprises are selling smart cars, and construction firms are pitching smart buildings, all converging on creating the smart cities of the future.

It is possible that your company has nothing to do with any of this, but it is becoming increasingly less likely. And if you are looking for secular growth, this is where it is most likely to come from. And most important, if those disruptions are beginning to swirl around you, there is never a more important time to embrace an outside-in perspective and planning process.

As Cisco's CEO, John Chambers, likes to say, "Market transitions wait for no one." Not for your customers. Not for your partners. Not for your competitors. And not for you. When the time comes, that sets the time. And just like when you were a kid playing hide and seek, there's a voice that comes out of nowhere calling, *"Ready or not, here I come!"*

ESCAPE
VELOCITY

CHAPTER ONE

Escape Velocity and the Hierarchy of Powers

To free your company's future from the pull of the past, to escape the gravitational field of your prior year's operating plan, and to complete the round-trip by returning with next year's operating plan, you need to apply a force that is greater than the inertial momentum of current operations. No experienced executive is likely to underestimate the amount of force required. It is, as we like to say in Silicon Valley, ginormous.

Newton taught us several centuries ago in his first law of motion, the one that covers inertia, that an object at rest tends to stay at rest and an object in motion tends to continue in the direction in which it is currently moving. The same goes for resource allocation.

When organizations begin their strategic planning effort by circulating last year's operating plan, they reinforce the inertial properties of the resources as currently allocated. This is not a good outcome, but to be frank, there is no help for it. You cannot really zero-base the budget every year, not in an enterprise of any size. So you have to assume this inertial force will be introduced into the process at some point.

What you *can* do, however, is get yourself and your colleagues out in front of it. Specifically, you can take the time to develop and bring to the table an *outside-in, market-centric perspective* that is so compelling and so well informed that it can counterbalance the inside-out company-centric orientation of last year's operating plan. This will help correct for the one huge, glaring flaw in that plan—the fact that *it's all about you!*

It is not about the world or the market or your customers or your partners or even your competitors. It is exclusively and solely about you and your revenue and earnings targets and your desired return on equity and your management objectives, and your operating metrics and your internal disposition of resources, and perhaps most influentially, about your comp plan. But step back and take stock. The world is more powerful than you. The market is more powerful than you. Your customers are more powerful than you. And the sum of all your partners and competitors—the ecosystem—is more powerful than you. And just to put the cap on it, nobody really cares about you except you. So given the enormous challenge of counterbalancing the inertial momentum of last year's plan, what do you say we tap into some of these external sources of power to give your company a boost?

To do this you must conduct a series of dialogues before opening resource-allocation discussions. In them you profile trends and opportunities that can create new sources of wealth for your customers and your company and can stake out the positions of power you want to occupy. This is not a new idea. What is new is the mechanism by which we propose to do it.

Most strategy dialogues end up with executives talking at cross-purposes because—and this is one of the dirty secrets of enterprise management—nobody knows exactly what is meant by *vision* and *strategy*, and no two people ever quite agree on which topics belong where. That is why, when you ask members of an executive team to describe and explain the corporate strategy, you so frequently get wildly different answers. We just don't have a good business discipline for converging on issues this abstract. And that does not bode well for setting a clear trajectory to achieve escape velocity.

This book intends to change that. Leveraging a model we call the Hierarchy of Powers, it will provide a map that will engage you and your colleagues in the various domains of power in a systematic and structured way, ensuring that the right questions get the right kind of answers at the right time and in the right sequence.

THE HIERARCHY OF POWERS

The Hierarchy of Powers is a framework of frameworks. It sizes up all economic competitions in relation to five types of economic power, organized in descending order from most general to most specific, as follows:

1. Category power
2. Company power
3. Market power
4. Offer power
5. Execution power

This hierarchy derives from taking an investor view of your company. The first decision investors make is what categories to invest in. Once they have determined that, then they choose specific companies. Once they hold stock in a company, they dig into the dynamics of the markets it serves, the competitiveness of its offers, and its track record for executing to the forecasts it provides. That covers the hierarchy top to bottom and explains why it is in the order it is.

Within this framework, think of each type of power as being made up of a set of vectors, arrows of force, each arrow headed in its own direction. Taken together, combining both within and across the various levels in the model, these vectors can align with one another to reinforce the sum total of power, or they can cancel each other out to reduce power to near zero. Thus you can be in a hot category and fail to execute, producing a near-zero result. Similarly, you can execute like crazy in a dying category and have an equally disappointing outcome. But when you get the powers aligned, when each is reinforcing the others, then the magic they call *synergy* appears, and very good things can happen indeed.

In this chapter we are going to summarize the forces incorporated at each level of the Hierarchy of Powers framework and call out the management issues that get addressed at that level. This will provide a road map for the rest of the book. Each of the subsequent five chapters will drill down into the dynamics of one of the five levels of power and present specific models to address the issues that pertain to that level, illustrating how they apply to particular situations and concluding with an extended case example to pull everything together. A concluding chapter will recap this material and describe how it can be integrated into an annual planning process that, yes, does include circulating last year's operating plan, but in the proper place and at the proper time.

For the rest of this introductory chapter, just sit back and get the lay of the land. As you read along, take some time to register how each type of power influences economic performance and think about the impact it might be having on your enterprise.

CATEGORY POWER

Category power is a function of the demand for a given class of products or services relative to all other classes. Categories in high demand, like smart phones, storage systems, and cloud computing, are more successful than their peers in securing customer budgets to fund them. Thus they grow faster and typically enjoy better profit margins. So participating in a powerful category is a very good thing indeed. Conversely, participating in a low-power category, such as desktop computers, wire-line phone services, or e-mail, is an exercise in playing on the margins. It can be quite profitable, but you definitely have to watch your step.

Being able to enter new categories and exit old ones is fundamental to freeing your company's future from the pull of the past—but it is not easy. Moreover, the challenges of maintaining a balanced portfolio of categories increase with the continued success of any franchise. Companies under $1 billion in revenue and under fifteen years or so in age typically have monolithic portfolios, made up of many products but all in the same category. It might be storage, or security software, or mobile devices, or enterprise resource planning (ERP). But at some later stage, typically through mergers and acquisitions, the corporation transforms into something more like a holding company, in which multiple heterogeneous categories combine to leverage a unified supply chain and a global sales and services footprint. This is when the fun starts.

Each category in a portfolio has its own unique dynamics. At the same time, however, the enterprise as a whole is held to a single report card for its collective performance, most visibly represented by its quarterly earnings. As an agent of the investors, the management team is responsible for maintaining a portfolio that maximizes quarterly returns over time. In this context, last year's plan inevitably favors the current portfolio, even when its quality may be deteriorating. And because it is a rare organization indeed that can decide to kill anything and an even rarer one that can actually succeed in doing so, deterioration is not an uncommon state of affairs.

To escape this gravitational field, you need to both objectively assess your current portfolio and identify credible category alternatives that are extremely compelling. This exercise usually goes by the name of *portfolio management* and is a standard part of an enterprise planning process. The core questions upon which it builds include:

- **Where is category growth contributing to our overall growth objectives?** Investors will pay a premium for revenue in these categories, so you want to maximize their share of your overall portfolio.

- **Where is lack of category growth inhibiting our growth objectives?** Investors discount this revenue, and so you want to minimize its share.
- **To the degree we participate in multiple categories, how well balanced is our overall portfolio in terms of contribution to current earnings, current growth, and future growth objectives?** Different strategies assign different weights to these three elements, so you want to make sure your weighting is consistent with your strategy.
- **In light of the above, do we need to enter a new category, divest ourselves from a category we are currently in, or stay the course with our current portfolio?** Executives often express envy about other businesses that are in higher-growth categories than they are, but the truth is, getting your company into the right categories is your responsibility as an executive.

Portfolio management questions are typically asked and answered once a year, with the expectation of staying the course in most years. Nevertheless, as experienced investors will tell you, category performance is the number-one predictor of company performance. No business can outperform its category over time. So being in the right categories at the right times is crucial to long-term success.

At the time of this writing, for example, Apple is enjoying exceptional financial returns, in part because it participates in a number of high-growth categories—smart phones, digital music distribution, and touch-screen tablets, to name three (all of which owe much of their fantastic growth to Apple's extraordinary innovations in each). At the same

time, Dell is struggling economically and, not coincidentally, participates in none of these categories. As a result,
it is in the process of repositioning itself as more of an enterprise company, competing against IBM and HP. On the
other hand, a decade ago the shoe was on the other foot.
Dell was the darling of the tech sector, right at the heart of
a vibrant PC category, and Apple was a marginalized and
fading star. That's how category power works. As the Beach
Boys used to sing, "Catch a wave and you're sittin' on top of
the world!"

But this raises a larger, darker question. What do you do when
you *know* you do not have the right mix of categories, when you
know you are missing out on a hot opportunity, when you *know*
you are clinging too long to a dying vine? Recall that litany of
gone but not forgotten enterprises from the previous chapter?
Those were not good companies—they were *great* companies.
So we must not underestimate the potential impact of being
unable to reallocate resources to enter and exit categories at
appropriate times.

And why would we be unable to? Because we are unable
to negotiate our collective release from the pull of the past
and the tyranny of last year's operating plan. That plan institutionalizes the current set of categories, granting each one
its allotment of resources, resources sufficiently in demand
to be jealously guarded. Thus we institutionalize a mentality
of scarcity, one that has no word of welcome for a newcomer.

So when we dig into category power, we will spend only a
little time on how to determine what categories we *should* be
in, and a whole lot of time on how to counteract the forces
that are keeping us from actually getting there.

COMPANY POWER

Within a given category, company power reflects the status and prospects of a specific vendor relative to its competitive set, power typically signaled by that company's market share. Note that the same enterprise can have different levels of company power in different categories, so total company power is based on the sum of the positions it has in the total set of categories that make up its revenues, multiplied by the power those categories have in their own right, as well as by whatever synergy there may be among them. This is the calculus of investor valuation, and as you may well appreciate, there is plenty of room for multiple points of view.

That said, all sectors of any size are characterized by three tiers of companies, of which the first tier are the ones with true company power. Thus in automotive, despite its many travails, General Motors is still a Tier 1 company, and despite all its recent success, Hyundai is still Tier 2. In high tech, there is a coterie of Tier 1 companies in enterprise IT, of which IBM, Oracle, HP, SAP, Cisco, EMC, Dell, Microsoft, and Accenture are particularly prominent, and another in consumer products and services, where Apple, Google, eBay, Yahoo!, Adobe, Amazon, and Facebook head the pack.

Tier 2 companies represent that portion of the rest of the category that has brand recognition—think Volvo in cars, Sony in PCs, LG in smart phones—while Tier 3 companies represent the unbranded: even when they may actually be producing a substantial portion of the category's overall volume, as they do in highly fragmented markets, they have little to no *company* power.

In this context, one of the key functions of escape velocity is to solve for the problem of moving up one tier, escaping the gravitational field of the one you are in, and bursting through the force fields that surround the one you are seeking to enter. Changing tiers means altering your strategic position relative to your competitive set. The focus of investment is on advantages that are ready to hand, current and active sources of power that can be leveraged in the present to change your state.

We call these sources of power *crown jewels.* These are unique assets and capabilities under your direct control that have the potential to confer on your company substantial and sustainable competitive advantage in the primary categories in which you participate or intend to participate. When it comes to managing or acquiring crown jewels that will truly support sustainable company power, there are a host of questions that must be addressed, including the following:

- **What exactly are our crown jewels, and are we investing enough to sustain or even increase their unique capabilities?** It is not uncommon for crown jewels to be underleveraged, buried under a load of more urgent but less important work.
- **Do our innovation investments focus on leveraging our crown jewels, or are we spreading ourselves too thin and failing to achieve genuine competitive separation?** The answer is almost universally the latter, which is actually a kind of good news, as it means there are readily available opportunities to improve.
- **Have we engineered our offers and our organization to leverage our crown jewels for maximum sustainable differentiation from our competitive**

set? The answer here normally is that we did so in the past but have fallen back into the pack of late. This is the inevitable result of the inertial forces we have been discussing. Again it bodes well for the likelihood that good opportunities exist.

- **Are we optimizing and economizing aggressively enough in areas that are not core to our defining differentiation?** Almost certainly not, as incumbent powers that be inevitably co-opt additional resources to protect against failing to meet their mission-critical responsibilities.

These are tough questions to tackle under the best of circumstances. They are virtually impossible to address when under the shadow of last year's operating plan. Once that becomes a baseline, it confers a level of entitlement to the status quo that is inherently incompatible with maximizing future competitive advantage. Uncritically following such a course leads inevitably to dilution of differentiation, erosion of competitive advantage, waste of innovation resources on things that don't matter (or more precisely, that don't matter enough), and failure to achieve sufficient competitive separation on the things that do matter. You end up doing far more things than you should and doing them far less well than you want.

Now, in mature markets with relatively stable market shares, such behavior tends to result in lackluster middle-of-the-pack results, not abject failure. But in the context of secular growth markets, such weak showings get shouldered aside in a hurry. If you are to compete here, your company must differentiate to such a degree that, for its target markets at least, your offers are simply unmatchable. And that means you have to allocate resources in a radically asymmetrical way, including outsourcing or partnering for huge chunks of your value chain that under less dynamic circumstances you would prefer to keep under your direct control.

Asymmetrical bets are the foundation for creating company power, putting in high relief the distinction between *leadership* and *management*. Managers resist asymmetrical bets for a host of good reasons: They are both inequitable and socially unpopular. They are hard for shared services organizations to support. They entail taking high-visibility (and potentially career-limiting) risks. They run roughshod over personal loyalties. They stretch the organization far beyond the limits of its comfort zone. They are departures from the norm.

Leaders acknowledge all of the above, but they still persist in making asymmetrical bets, also for a host of good reasons: They want the power to win. They are more externally than internally focused. They want to adapt the company to the market, not the other way around. They want to make a difference. They want to make sure that sacrifices—which are inevitable in any strategy—are made in a worthwhile cause.

If you expect to achieve company power, you must *lead first* and *manage second*. Companies unable to achieve escape velocity have almost always fallen into the opposite cadence of manage first, lead second. This is an easy habit to fall into, for it is the inevitable result of focusing the bulk of your time, talent, and attention on yourselves. Thus it was that HP managed to miss the Internet during the 1990s, being focused instead on expanding its successes in traditional client-server computing. It just wasn't clear where the Internet money would come from. Ironically, the decade before, it was the prodding leadership of executives like Bernard Guidon that got HP into client-server systems in the first place. The managers of that era could not see letting go of their bird-in-the-hand higher-margin proprietary minicomputer franchises, fragmented and low-growth though they were, because it wasn't absolutely clear where the two-in-the-bush money was going to come from.

And HP is hardly alone in this behavior. Indeed, the whole challenge of the pull of the past is that it always makes good management sense to go with it. There is rarely a time when changing direction offers a better risk-adjusted short-term return than staying the course. How else to explain how Xerox could have failed to capitalize on all the innovation coming out of its Palo Alto Research Center? How else to explain how the Motorola people could have failed to put out an iPhone-like phone in the several years prior to Apple when they had all the technology and know-how necessary?

Although this problem is common and vexing, the path to reform is nonetheless clear. Spend more time, talent, and attention—a whole lot more—on things outside yourselves, be they customers, partners, competitors, technology changes, or market shifts. Find in these external forces the things to lead the company toward, and then turn over to management the task of getting the company safely there. Leadership is about being in service to a higher cause; management is about ensuring that service is appropriately rewarded. Both are necessary. You just can't put the focus on rewards first.

MARKET POWER

Market power is company power within the confines of a single market segment. Market segments are defined as sets of customers who share a common and unique set of needs and who reference each other, directly or indirectly, when making their purchase decisions. Market power is measured by word-of-mouth reputation within this community of reference and is confirmed by market share specific to that segment.

Market power is highly desirable in two distinct types of situations. The first is when markets are in transition. At such times significant chunks of customer budget float free from their moorings as the businesses in the segment try to come to terms with some disruptive change. Segments in this state seek a return to stability as soon as possible but cannot get there until an agreed-upon solution from an agreed-upon set of preferred vendors has emerged. Segment-focused initiatives by a vendor during the transition period can accelerate this process and capture the desired lead position, resulting in sustainable market power, significant downstream revenues, and highly attractive profit margins.

The other type of situation where market power can be transformative is when companies have stumbled or a competitor has stolen a march on them. Relegated now to the middle of the pack, and frankly at risk of falling still further, these companies can rally their troops and supporters around a newly gained market-segment leadership position, repositioning themselves as niche market leaders in vibrant new market segments. Once again the value-creating state is to be the undisputed leader in the segment.

Market power, like political power in electoral politics, is a territory capture game. Ecosystems prefer to organize around an established leader at the head of a known pecking order. Company power establishes the global pecking order, but individual markets frequently cast their votes for a different candidate. Market-segment leaders are perceived to be the safe buy within the targeted segment and as such enjoy sustainable competitive advantages over all other vendors, including the overall category leader with a much bigger share of the category as a whole. Thus while Oracle leads in the database category overall, Sybase dominates on Wall Street. And while Cisco is the clear category leader in switching and routing, Juniper has the lead in the telecommunications segment. And when SAP took the ERP category by storm, Lawson Software, though much smaller, was able to stake out the number-one position in U.S. health care.

These local victories can be highly lucrative in their own right as well as contribute to a broader campaign for moving company power to a new tier. As with presidential primaries, however, coming in second in a niche market is of little to no value. The simple lesson here: focus works. Anybody can be the big fish by picking a pond of appropriate size and then delivering a value proposition unmatchable by the rest of the competitive set.

When pursuing a strategy of market-segment focus, there are any number of questions that challenge executives:

- **Is the market segment big enough to matter, yet small enough to win decisively?** This is the presidential-primary question. It means that market segmentation needs to produce red state/blue state maps, with swing states highlighted.
- **Are our market-specific commitments sufficiently focused and intense to win market power?** This leads to follow-on questions like, Can we afford to make these commitments? And the balancing question, Can we afford not to?

- **Are we winning fast enough?** The answer is typically no, and this leads to the follow-on question, What can we do to accelerate our progress?
- **Are we making the market sufficiently lucrative for our partners so that they will proactively participate in completing our whole offer?** In a disaggregated economy, ecosystem support is critical to gaining and sustaining competitive advantage, yet few companies give enough attention to the health of their partners.
- **Are we capturing a price premium commensurate with the unique value proposition we provide?** Market power is expensive to field, so it must generate above-average returns to fuel the effort.
- **Do we have a clear line of sight to our growth opportunities in adjacent market segments?** For companies of global size, a single niche market will not generate material returns, but one that serves as a head bowling pin for knocking down additional segments changes the math.

Once again we see that strategy to gain power rests upon willingness to allocate resources in highly asymmetrical ways, exchanging a smaller short-term gain for a larger mid-term return. As with all gains based on deferral, it turns out that the challenge with market power is not so much how to get it but how to motivate ourselves and our investors sufficiently to make the commitment to go out and do so. To make that commitment, management and investors must concur that a dollar of revenue won from the target segment is worth more—indeed, considerably more—than a dollar won from the world at large.

The rationale for this claim is that such a dollar, added to more dollars from the same segment, contributes toward what Malcolm Gladwell has taught us to call a tipping-point outcome, a moment of transition in which customers in the segment move en masse to the new offer and its preferred vendor. Once this tipping point is reached, a flood of market interest is released from this segment and adjacent ones, and it comes at a dramatically lower cost of marketing, leading in turn to revenue gained at a dramatically lower cost of sales. There is plenty of evidence that this phenomenon is real and can be engineered through a focused effort. But you have to commit the resources to get it done, and it takes tough dialogue to get there.

Trying to conduct this dialogue in the context of a budget negotiation organized around last year's operating plan is simply a nonstarter. That puts too many hungry mouths at the table, each with a head start at claiming a share of the dishes being passed. And every one of those mouths is counting on, or at least hoping for, the sales and marketing team to help bring home its bacon. Imagine their reaction when a new kid comes to the table and asks for some exclusive sales resources just for a single specific segment, and not a very large one at that. Knives come out faster than business cards at a trade show.

By contrast, however, if you can front-end the budgeting process with a strategy dialogue organized around the Hierarchy of Powers, then you can make sure market-power opportunities get a thorough vetting and a fair hearing. They still have to compete for resources, but they can do so in the context of having their unique assets fully in view instead of obscured or suppressed, as they must inherently be if they are filtered through the tables and spreadsheets of a prior year's analysis.

OFFER POWER

Offer power is a function of the demand for a given product or service relative to its reference competitors. In mature categories the reference base is simply the competitive set that makes up the category. In emerging categories it also extends to status quo alternatives that are not in the same category but compete for the same budget.

Offer power is most prominent in the strategies of volume-operations enterprises, for the transactional nature of these businesses inevitably leaves the offer to fend more or less for itself. At the time of this writing, Apple's iPhone has used offer power to achieve escape velocity in spades, leaving both Motorola and Nokia scrambling for an "iPhone killer." Google search achieved escape velocity earlier in the decade, as did Facebook's social network. Groupon's daily deals have achieved escape velocity, but it remains to be seen how sustainable that competitive separation will be. Microsoft Office had what once was thought to be insurmountable competitive separation, but lately it is getting commoditized by "good enough" alternatives from Google and others, threatening to suck it back into a competitive set. Ditto for Research in Motion's BlackBerry, HP's inkjet printers, Cisco Linksys's home routers, and Dell's laptops.

As these examples illustrate, offer power is perhaps the most transient of all the powers in the hierarchy. It wasn't that long ago that Nokia's offers were the wonder of the world, not to mention Sony's Walkman or Sega's Sonic the Hedgehog. In volume-operations businesses, you are only as good as your latest hit. Hits—like a Microsoft Office, an Intuit QuickBooks, or an Autodesk AutoCAD—are what create the center of a brand franchise, one that can drag along hosts of ancil-lary less differentiated offers.

Of course, if you ever were fortunate enough to actually get a hit, surely it would not be hard to capitalize on it down-stream, right? Well, Lotus was never able to do it with its 1-2-3 spreadsheet, nor was Motorola successful in following up either its StarTac or its Razr hit phones. So why do we think these products failed to establish lasting franchises?

One reason was that they were unable to win a dispropor-tionate share of the resources allocated in the years following their hit performance. Competing projects were too deeply entrenched in the politics of the organization to be uprooted. There was no mechanism by which to declare that a dollar invested in line extensions from the hit would create more offer power than it would invested in any of the less distin-guished alternatives. And there were plenty of social mecha-nisms that argued for equitable distribution, giving each a fair chance, not playing favorites.

Unfortunately, economic success depends deeply on play-ing favorites, of making starkly asymmetrical bets. That's why it is so important to have a strategic dialogue prior to resource-allocation decisions. You have to nominate the favor-ites, fight fiercely about which ones are truly deserving, and drive yourselves to the edge. That's how you escape the gravi-tational field of your competitive set. And to do that, you have to escape the gravitational field of last year's operating plan.

For executives facing such challenges, the questions that most need answering are:

- **Is this offer a proven hit, a potential hit, or more of a product-line filler?** All three may well be worth funding, but surely not equally.

- **Is this offer sufficiently differentiated to gain escape velocity from its competitive set?** If so, for which customers and on what basis?
- **What can we do to amplify its differentiation further?** What can we do to make it truly unmatchable, thereby extending its effective life and the life of the franchise it anchors?
- **Where are we wasting resources majoring in minors or chasing a competitor's tail?** How soon can we stop, so we can fund the offers that we really want to rally behind?

At the end of the day, offer power is not just about revenue. Any product can generate some revenue and, properly managed, can do so at a profit. But only a few products can generate the kind of force that causes whole markets to reconfigure, thereby causing the products around them to be valued more highly. It is quite possible that you have no such products in your portfolio today. But that is no reason not to create some for tomorrow.

EXECUTION POWER

Execution power is the ability to outperform your competitive set under conditions that favor no vendor in particular. For the most part, it is focused on your existing book of business and thus is more about securing the present than freeing your future. For this reason, execution is often set in opposition to strategy, much the way that practice is set opposite theory or the real world is set opposite an imagined one.

A focus on escape velocity reframes this relationship dramatically. In this context we are talking not about execution in general but rather *the ability to execute a game-changing shift in operating priorities.* In this context, traditional execution skills may be more part of the problem than of the solution.

So what does it take to execute an escape-velocity strategy? Basically, three things:

1. You must innovate sufficiently to achieve competitive separation. This is the domain of invention.
2. You must institutionalize the activities that underlie that separation so that it can be scaled and sustained. This is the domain of deployment.
3. You must drive the transition from invention to deployment to a tipping point such that the world will go forward as newly aligned and not fall back into its old ways.

How matters unfold takes on a different cast depending on whether your company has more of a B2B complex-systems model or takes more of a B2C volume-operations approach. In the former, execution of innovation foregrounds *project* capabilities, specifically the ability to engage a visionary customer with a custom services model and end up with an output that can be repurposed for other customers and, at least to some degree, standardized. That act of standardizing is what institutionalizes competitive separation. We call it transitioning from *project* to *playbook*, and we will have a great deal to say about this trajectory later on in the book.

Once the playbook has been captured, complex-systems offers can be scaled, and competitors can be left behind. Thus Cisco's StadiumVision team conducted projects with the Dallas Cowboys and the New York Yankees to show what was possible and is now working with a second wave of customers to institutionalize these capabilities into a playbook for general rollout. Thus Adobe has done projects with early adopters in several sectors to show what its Customer Engagement Management software can do to change the dynamics of a consumer relationship; now the company is institutionalizing this offer in playbooks for financial services and health care.

Playbooks thus are pivotal to executing for escape velocity. Unfortunately, they are also an unnatural act for most enterprises. Complex-systems sales forces love to sell what the customer wants, and this inevitably depositions the playbook solution, causing it to slide back into a custom project. And engineering teams love the challenge of a new project since this allows them to further exercise their invention muscles. And to add insult to injury, it turns out that playbooks themselves are very hard to write, tending to fail in one of two extremes—a three-pager that is nowhere specific enough or fifty-plus pages that bore to tears.

In B2C enterprises, escape velocity takes on a more external, market-facing cast. Invention is achieved through introducing an innovative offer, be it a product or service, something that catches the attention of consumers and hooks them as retained users or repeat buyers, be that on daily, weekly, monthly, or annual basis. Think Facebook, Mad Men, HP inkjet cartridges, or the latest Kindle from Amazon.

In this context, the transition from invention to broadly scaled deployment is a race against time to get past the tipping point that separates the hits from the flops. It is a race that cannot be won without help: the critical determinant of

B2C success is the enterprise's ability to recruit partners to extend its reach and complete its value proposition.

These partnerships take on many forms. In the case of a media property like Yahoo! or AOL, they are with other publishers to syndicate content and with brand advertisers to monetize the overall effort. With consumer gadgets like SkyGolf's SkyCaddie or TomTom's personal navigation devices, it is all about winning the support of the golf courses or points of traveler interest, along with getting shelf space in retail distribution outlets. In the case of electronic platforms like Apple's iOS or Google's Android, it takes an ecosystem of software developers to transform these innovations' value into consumable benefits. And finally, even in the case of free offers, be they an open source product or a cool new game or site, mass distribution is a function of enlisting others to carry the message for you. This is the whole point behind social media and viral marketing.

In every case in the volume-operations model, the transition from invention to deployment requires an external-facing, market-engaging, partner-recruiting effort—something worlds apart from the internal-facing transition of project to playbook that complex systems teams must go through. And it is here where so many B2C efforts go awry. The inventors want the scaling effort to be all about the product when in fact it is mostly about the people outside your enterprise and their willingness to be co-opted into your effort.

Stepping back from whether one is scaling a complex-systems or a volume-operations offering, in either case the simple act of transitioning itself is an unnatural act for most organizations. Once they get established in a given execution mode, they don't want to change. Thus the real key to achieving escape velocity is to overlay an additional execution discipline, *transition programs*, the role of which is to convert an activity from a current to a future state, be that from process to playbook (complex systems) or from product to partners (volume operations).

Transition programs, in this context, are vehicles for driving organizations to tipping points. That is not how most other programs are normally chartered—"best efforts" are the more common standard—but in an escape-velocity scenario, there can be no compromise. If you do not get to the tipping point, you have wasted your program budget, disappointed your customers and partners, and given up a tempo to the competition. Conversely, if you do get to the tipping point, every task you have been laboring to perform up to that point becomes remarkably easier, indeed miraculously so. You have crested a hill, and now instead of pedaling with all your might, you are coasting free and feeling glorious.

All in all, there are four execution modes—the two that are key to escape velocity, *invention* and *deployment*; a third that is key to mature markets, *optimization*; and a fourth focused on managing the handoffs among the other three, *transition programs*. We will dig into the dynamics of each and their relationships with one another when we come to chapter 6. For now it is enough to register the issues and questions that arise when enterprises focus on execution power:

- **Are we clear about the state of each of our lines of business and the corresponding execution mode that should be foregrounded?** Organizations tend to privilege what they are best at, not necessarily what is required. To a man with a hammer, everything looks like a nail.

- **Do we have the right kinds of leaders in charge, given the execution discipline that is required?** Again, organizations tend to leave the same people in place for the life of a line of business, which is often not good either for the business or the people.
- **Have we highlighted the lines of business that are in transition, either from invention to deployment (the escape-velocity transition) or from deployment to optimization (the maturation transition)?** These are the times of greatest risk to lose power, and it is critical that everyone pay close attention until the transitions are complete.
- **With respect to the transition programs, do we have clear milestones and metrics and visibility to ensure we know when they have reached their tipping points?** The answer here is almost certainly "not today," as this is a novel idea. But it is essential to install these disciplines if your enterprise is to achieve its highest ambitions.

Execution initiatives in support of escape velocity run in parallel with ongoing execution in support of the status quo, and neither should be allowed to compromise the other. Nonetheless, they do compete with each other for time, talent, and management attention, especially at the top of the organization. When that happens, escape-velocity initiatives must come first. If your organization cannot perform its ongoing execution responsibilities without your constant supervision, then you have bigger problems to tackle than this one.

SUMMING UP

Stepping back from all that we have covered in this chapter, you can see that the Hierarchy of Powers covers an enormous amount of ground. It should not be surprising, therefore, given all the different issues in play, that strategy dialogues frequently get off track and lose their way. At the same time, it is hard to see how your enterprise could develop a robust strategy, one sufficiently grounded to compete with the status quo for next year's operating resources, without covering all these bases. And should you fall short of that goal, it is hard to see how you can achieve the escape velocity needed to free your company's future from the pull of the past.

So we have reached a good stepping-off point. If you don't buy into the arguments you have encountered in this chapter, then let me thank you for giving me your attention thus far, and let us part on good terms. If, on the other hand, you do buy in or at least are curious enough to proceed, now would be a good time to buckle your seat belt, because we are about to dive into the maelstrom of topics and issues and anxieties and turbulence that these models inevitably raise.

Welcome aboard.

CHAPTER TWO

Category Power: Reengineering Portfolio Management

t is the fall of 2010, and this year two iconic brands in the world of print media, *Businessweek* and *Newsweek,* have each been sold at an extraordinary price—rumored to be $1 apiece! Meanwhile 3Par, a not particularly distinguished storage company, has been acquired for $2.3 billion, ten times last year's trailing revenues. As the kids like to ask, What's up with that?

Welcome to the world of category power. Print media are falling off the end of the category maturity life cycle, being displaced everywhere by digital media. When this happens, it doesn't matter how good your brand is—just ask Kodak what happened to its brand when film got displaced by digital photography. Meanwhile that same shift to digital media has thrust the storage category onto a massive secular growth curve. Timing is everything.

Category power, in short, is the number-one predictor of future economic performance. So if you are going to free your future from the pull of the past, this is the place to begin. The exercise goes by the name of portfolio management, and it begins with the category maturity life cycle.

CATEGORY POWER AND THE CATEGORY MATURITY LIFE CYCLE

The fundamental model for understanding the dynamics of category power is the category maturity life cycle. This model has been at the center of my life's work and will be highly familiar to readers of prior books (see, in particular, *Dealing with Darwin*, chapter 2). Here I want to use it to focus on the *changes in state* categories pass through over their life cycle, and the implications of these state changes for the future of your franchise.

Category power manifests itself in five different states, represented in Figure 2.1 by the letters A to E. The significance of these states is as follows:

A. Emerging Categories

These are the maelstroms in which new wealth-creating engines are born. They are governed by the Technology Adoption Life Cycle, the dynamics of which are dealt with in depth in two prior books, *Crossing the Chasm* and *Inside the Tornado* (see, in particular, *Inside the Tornado*, chapter 2).

Category Maturity Life Cycle

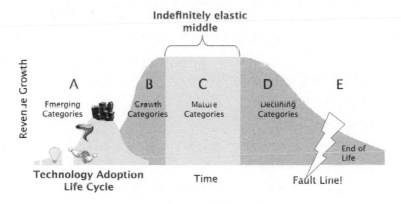

Figure 2.1

For established enterprises, emerging categories are a real challenge. They entail high risks combined with highly variable rewards, demand a lot of attention from top-flight resources, but do not provide material returns in the near term. All this runs directly counter to the expectations investors have for current-quarter performance gains from publicly held companies. There are still corner cases where it makes sense for established companies to play, but only under conditions we will specify later and only when combined with a specialized management approach we will spell out in detail.

For start-ups, on the other hand, emerging categories are a godsend. They put the incumbents in their weakest possible position and create openings for no-name disrupters. Individual odds of success are not high, but the portfolio approach built into the venture capital model allows investors to get a great return from just a handful of winners. As a result, a large population of start-ups gets funded, and this is a critical source of innovation for global commerce.

Overall, Stage A represents category power in its most volatile state. This is goodness for the barbarians at the gate and badness for the guardians of the status quo.

B. Growth Categories

These are the great wealth-creation vehicles for public enterprises. Growth in a Stage B category is a secular one-time-only affair. New customers are coming into the market with new money, and a market share land grab is under way, but it is not yet certain who will be the winner. As a result, all companies in the category get an "option value" valuation bonus from investors based on the possibility of their becoming that winner. That's why price-earnings ratios are highest during this phase of the life cycle. It represents category power in its happiest state.

In Stage B category competitions, established enterprises have powerful competitive advantages over new entrants. Their global footprints for sales and services give them far superior market access, and their brand credibility shortens sales cycles and helps them get the final nod. Thus it is no accident that venture-backed enterprises are increasingly glad to get acquired during this stage, and more and more management teams actually stay past their earn-outs in order to play out their category visions on a larger stage.

On the other hand, if the incumbents deny the new paradigm and persist in their loyalty to the status quo, or if that new paradigm becomes global overnight (as is now possible in digital media businesses, for example), then the trumpets blow, the world order is destabilized, and the walls come tumbling down. This is the time of Joseph Schumpeter's *creative destruction*, and in the past decade or so it has struck not only film photography and print media but also retail bookselling, music distribution, TV and movies, and cell phones. If you are not on the right side of category power, you will see its dark side instead.

The overall rhythm of innovation in a secular growth market is *invent, test—learn, deploy, redeploy—reinvent*. There is no time for *optimize*—that will come when the market finally matures. For now, it's a land grab for which there are two basic rules:

1. *Must be present to win* (you have to be in the game regardless, which leads to a codicil rule of *Go ugly early*); and
2. *Best offer carries the day* (which is fundamentally a deployment strategy that vows not to lose the deal, regardless).

Both of these rules play to the advantage of start-ups and "first growth" companies riding their initial success in the category maturity life cycle. Neither of them, by contrast, is appropriate for operating in a mature market, which is one of the big reasons why there is so much internal friction when a single enterprise has major opportunities in both Stage B and Stage C of the life cycle.

C. Mature Categories

This is where the overwhelming bulk of the world's economic returns are generated year after year. It is also where the vast majority of jobs and tax returns are generated. In short, Stage C categories are the bulwark of society worldwide.

Mature categories offer stability and predictability. Market leadership positions change very slowly, and established enterprises dominate. Growth is cyclical. If you miss out in one round, you can pick it up in the next one. In addition, you can acquire your way back into any game you lost out in, using the efficiencies of consolidation to pay back the acquisition capital deployed.

All of this is not lost on investors, who historically have bought and held stocks in mature categories, seeking short-term dividend income, long-term modest appreciation, and low risk. The overall rhythm of innovation appropriate to these aspirations is *optimize, learn, invent, deploy, optimize—repeat*. That may not sound very innovative to you, but it is how you capitalize on cyclical growth. Stage C category victories go to the tortoises, not the hares.

D. Declining Categories

These are categories that have transitioned from cyclical growth rates to persistently negative ones. This is a secular change, meaning it is only going to get worse. That said, like many things in life, it may take a long time to get a lot worse. And in that thought lies the art of managing Stage D category positions.

Established enterprises are the only players of merit at this stage. The market is not looking for new vendors; rather it is deciding whether to bite the bullet on changing out infrastructure now or to stretch its current position for a little longer. There is real value to customers or consumers in doing the latter if the category in question is not core to their business or lifestyle. As a result, there can be a convergence of high value, low risk, and low need for investment, all of which can make Stage D the most profitable of any stage in the life cycle. It's a bit like leaving the grapes on the vine so long that they begin to rot, then turning them into a fine sauterne.

Public-market investors, however, discount the prospects for Stage D businesses and assign them little to no value in assessing your overall portfolio. As a result, management teams do not talk about them much but do tuck in their earnings to prop up overall financial performance. The problem with this trick is that each quarter you have to show growth, and each quarter Stage D businesses shrink, so sooner or later you are going to have a miss and the painful adjustment in stock price that comes with it.

Private-equity buyout firms, by contrast, have no such problems. They love Stage D businesses because they can take them over, shut down all investments in the future, play out the present assets as profitably as possible, and either pack up the leftovers to sell or shut the thing down. The rhythm of innovation here is *optimize, optimize, optimize—repeat*. While requiring a lot of work, much of which is socially painful, this represents a very low-risk approach to generating relatively high returns.

The key point for us to take away is that in Stage D, for the first time, category power is a negative force. We are swimming against the tide. In the short term, this may winnow out our competitors before it gets to us, so there are some compensations, but overall, when you factor in the time, talent, and management attention any business must consume, it is

normally better for established enterprises to divest themselves of Stage D assets early and repurpose their assets into
categories that are at an earlier stage.

E. End of Life

This phase is the end of a category's commercial viability,
as in telegrams, telexes, rotary phones, movie projectors,
slide rules, typewriters, carbon paper, Wite-Out, jukebox-
es, transistor radios, rabbit-ear antennae, carburetors, and
the like. A category reaching end of life has been known
to cripple an entire enterprise's viability, which is nothing
short of tragic. This happens when a company stays too
long at the fair.

Staying too long means continuing to invest in Stage D
categories in order to extend their life cycles just a little bit
longer. Kodak's last foray into next-generation film, Polaroid's
little tiny pictures, and Blockbuster Video's brick-and-mortar-
only expansion initiatives are three examples. These were all
companies where management at the time knew they were in
category trouble but simply could not see any place else to go.

Experience has taught us, however, there is *always* some-
place else to go. It's just that you have to jettison a lot of baggage to get yourself under way. And the longer you stay at the
fair, the more baggage you have to jettison and the weaker you
are when you start out. In short, Stage E is category power at
its most lethal. This is why it is so important for enterprises
to divest during Stage D—and relatively early in that stage
whenever possible.

Now, having surveyed the landscape of category power end
to end, it doesn't take a genius to realize what you would wish

for, namely a consistent cycle of innovation in Stage B, maturing into enduring franchises in Stage C, fed by the occasional foray into Stage A, fueled with the assets gained from divesting businesses in Stage D, all the while maintaining a "no fly zone" over Stage E. That is the theory of portfolio management in a nutshell.

The problem is not that management teams in established enterprises do not understand this goal. It is that they do not fully appreciate the forces that resist their achieving it and thus find themselves repeatedly in unbalanced, undesirable portfolio positions. Therefore, it is to those forces and the ways in which they can be counteracted that we shall now turn our attention.

THE GROWTH/MATERIALITY MATRIX: ASSESSING CATEGORY POWER

The clearest picture of your category power comes from placing your portfolio of businesses on the Growth/Materiality Matrix (see Figure 2.2).

To begin with, let's clarify the terms involved. By what benchmark do we determine if a category is high growth versus low growth? The simple answer is that growth of 15 percent to 30 percent (or more) is high and single-digit growth is low, the 10-to-15 percent range being a kind of a "tweener" zone.

These numbers come from inferring what rates of growth it takes to attract growth investors, as opposed to value investors. They also come from comparing secular growth rates in Stage B categories to cyclical growth rates in Stage C categories. What they emphatically *do not* come from is comparison

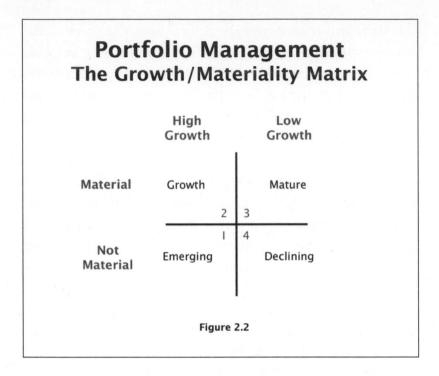

Figure 2.2

with the other businesses in your portfolio. This is key, so let's give it a bit more attention.

Suppose growth rates in your portfolio average 4 percent but you have one business that is 8 percent. Shouldn't that be treated as high growth? Absolutely not! Instead it should be treated as a comparison of two or more Stage C categories, one of which may or may not have more category power than its peers. (Remember, growth in mature markets is cyclical, so it could be one is up and the other down just for the current year.) The key point is that none of these categories has the kind of Stage B power that it takes to drive high growth. That is, none of them represent a secular growth market in which share battles result in new market leaders. And because they do not, they should not be resourced as if they did.

With that principle clearly in view, let's turn to the other axis in the matrix. By what benchmark do we determine if a category is material or not? Here it *is* by comparison to the other businesses in your portfolio. And the more material it is, the more it outshines those other businesses, the more power it has in resource-allocation negotiations during the annual budget process.

The rule of thumb we suggest for you to treat a category as material to your business is that it should generate 5 to 10 percent of either your total revenue or your total profit or should be expected to shortly. At this level of materiality, a business can normally get the full attention of the line functions responsible for making the current-quarter forecasts. Anything less than this is liable to be treated as a distraction.

With these clarifications in mind, let's now turn our atten-

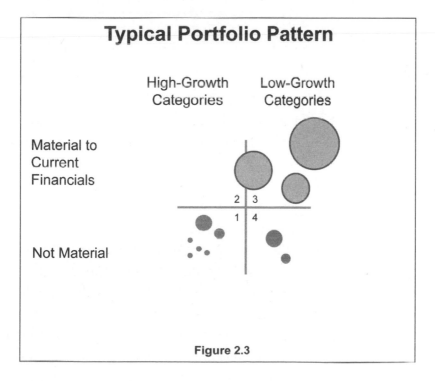

Typical Portfolio Pattern

High-Growth Categories   Low-Growth Categories

Material to Current Financials

Not Material

Figure 2.3

tion to a portfolio pattern that is typical of an established enterprise (see Figure 2.3).

Before we get down to specific cases, let's describe what this diagram is illustrating. An enterprise with this pattern is marked by highly material franchises in Stage C of the category maturity life cycle, represented by the large bubbles in quadrant 3. These are solid businesses and often exceptionally good earners. At the same time this company also has numerous investments in emerging high-growth categories, none of which as yet has become material, corresponding to the tiny bubbles in quadrant 1. It typically also has some hanger-on businesses, which are neither material nor high growth but still profitable, sometimes highly so, corresponding to the modest to small bubbles in quadrant 4, often in Stage D of the life cycle. Finally, most salient to this discussion, it typically has *no* material positions in high-growth categories, no significant Stage B plays, corresponding to quadrant 2.

In 2010 this describes some of the finest corporations in the history of high tech, including Microsoft, Intel, IBM, Oracle, HP, SAP, and Dell. All these companies have world-class franchises in mature Stage C categories—PC operating systems, microprocessors, IT consulting, enterprise applications, or the like. All of them are able to renew growth in these franchises on a cyclical basis, based on next-generation product releases in the same categories they currently dominate. None of them, however, in the past decade or more has been able to organically produce a major franchise that is Stage B. To be sure, all have invested heavily during this period to fund R&D for next-generation technologies, but these businesses have remained resolutely stuck in quadrant 1, unable to transition to quadrant 2, meaning they are high growth but always off a small base, proving unable to reach material size before management attention wanders or the axe falls.

By contrast, Figure 2.3 does not describe Apple, Google, NetApp, Cognizant, Sybase, or Cisco. What distinguishes the second group from the first is that every company in it has introduced at least one category into its portfolio in the past decade that has become both high growth and significantly material to the business. Apple is the darling of this set, participating in a plethora of Stage B quadrant 2 categories largely of its own devising. That is what makes it the most remarkable business story of the decade—even more impressive than Google's Android or Cisco's telepresence because it has brought not one but three net new material franchises into play all within the same decade.

Now let's be clear. In high tech, at least, every company has an ambition to do what Apple did, and in many cases they have very real opportunities to do so. Moreover, all of them have done it at least once before, or they would not be where they are today. So why doesn't it happen more often? Why do we find the cupboard of quadrant 2 so often bare?

The simple answer is that category portfolio management involves balancing different classes of investment, one against the other. These investments pay off in different time periods, and as a result conflicts of interest arise that interfere with executing a portfolio strategy. This is the essence of what Clay Christensen has taught us to call the innovator's dilemma. As he points out, there are no villains here, only persistently bad outcomes. So if we are going to meet this challenge head-on, it behooves us to get a very firm grasp on the dynamics in play.

PORTFOLIO INTERESTS IN CONFLICT: THE THREE HORIZONS MODEL

The easiest way to visualize the underlying problem that undermines most portfolio strategies is to apply the filter of the Three Horizons model presented by Mehrdad Baghai and his colleagues at McKinsey in *The Alchemy of Growth* (Figure 2.4).

The model calls out three different investment horizons, each promising a return in a different time period:

- **Horizon 1** investments are expected to contribute to material returns in the same fiscal year in which they are brought to market, thereby generating today's cash flow.

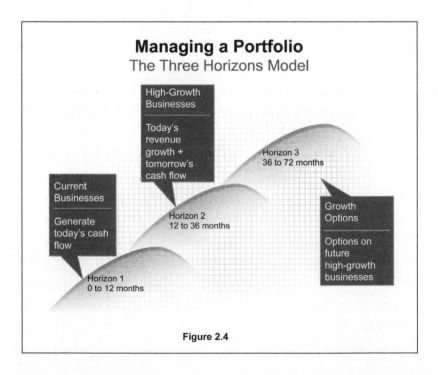

Managing a Portfolio
The Three Horizons Model

High-Growth Businesses

Today's revenue growth + tomorrow's cash flow

Horizon 3
36 to 72 months

Current Businesses

Generate today's cash flow

Horizon 2
12 to 36 months

Growth Options

Options on future high-growth businesses

Horizon 1
0 to 12 months

Figure 2.4

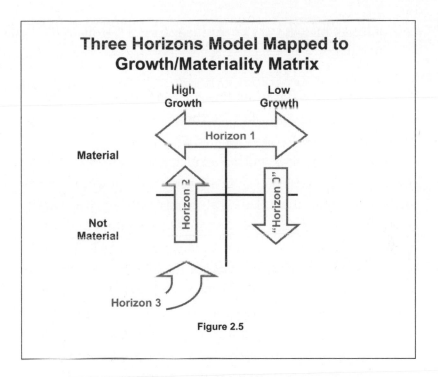

Three Horizons Model Mapped to Growth/Materiality Matrix

Figure 2.5

- **Horizon 2** investments are expected to pay back significantly, but not in the year of their market launch. Typically they are fast growing from birth but come off a small base and need time to reach a material size. Moreover, because market adoption is rarely linear, there are often fits and starts before they catch fire. In the meantime, however, they are making material demands on go-to-market resources in the current year without generating corresponding material returns, and so they demand patience.

- **Horizon 3** investments are investments in future businesses that will pay off in the out years beyond the current planning horizon. They are not expected to appear in market during the current planning year, and thus while they make claims against R&D

budgets, they do not affect the go-to-market operating plan.

Now if we map the three horizons onto the Growth/Materiality Matrix, we can see how they intersect with portfolio management (see Figure 2.5).

As the diagram makes clear, all material results occur in Horizon 1, and the Horizon 1 management team is accountable for making these numbers. This is always a challenge, particularly as the overall portfolio ages and pressure mounts to do more with less. As a result, Horizon 1 managers jealously guard the resources they have been given for the job and are not above co-opting any other resources they can lay their hands on to boot. In so doing they are *not* behaving badly. Indeed, it is a hallmark of superior Horizon 1 managers that they are able to secure contingency resources to meet the vagaries of a competitive marketplace. Darwin selects for this behavior.

That all said, this does not bode well for Horizon 2 initiatives. They have been charged to *become* material, which means they must make claims on the same resources targeted by the Horizon 1 managers. At the same time, their businesses *are not yet* material, meaning the current-year return on deploying those Horizon 1 resources is substantially below par.

Why is this so? Simply put, it takes many more resources to generate a dollar of revenue in Horizon 2 than it does in Horizon 1. Category demand and company reputation are not yet established, so the skids have not yet been greased. Moreover, the field sales personnel are not as familiar with the new product, nor are their established customer and prospect contacts likely to be the targeted buyers for it. Domain expertise is scarce to nonexistent, and partners are holding back in a wait-and-see mode.

Is it any wonder, then, that Horizon 2 initiatives get short shrift from Horizon 1 resources, especially when the Horizon 1 management team is measured first and foremost on making its materiality commitments?

Now note that Horizon 3 initiatives are exempt from this challenge. They are not expected to become material in the current period, and thus they make no claims on the Horizon 1 market-facing teams. Indeed, they are often paraded in front of Horizon 1 prospects as indicative of great things to come. And because they are unavailable today, they do not compete for Horizon 1 customer dollars. But this is not the case for Horizon 2 initiatives. They do ship today, and they can distract the prospect's attention and derail a more conventional offer currently on the table. So that's another strike against them.

But there's more. Horizon 2 offers are immature and thus, as end-to-end solutions, incomplete. To fulfill the promise they make to the customer, they must be complemented with professional services to complete the whole offer. These services must be discounted because, in effect, they are back-filling for things the customer has already been promised. Moreover, building out the whole offer for the first time is iffy work and tends to be underspecified. The Horizon 1 professional services team has revenue and contribution margin numbers of its own to hit. And these numbers are much easier to make by fulfilling established demand for conventional tasks. So that's another strike against Horizon 2.

And finally, put yourself in the marketing VP's shoes. You know that marketing's efforts are critical to help the Horizon 2 initiatives cross their chasm, but your resources are funded as a percent of total revenue, and the Horizon 1 team—your primary source of funding—is breathing down your neck for more leads—and good leads this time, not like that dreck that was sent over last time. You really do want to help the Horizon 2 team, but you can't cost-justify the intense and tightly targeted commitment that is actually required. So you do your best to tuck in the Horizon 2 messaging where you can. This has nothing like the impact needed, so that is yet another strike against the initiative.

Well, if you have been counting, you know we have already exceeded the "three strikes and you're out" rule. Thus it comes to pass that the dynamics of go-to-market execution—specifically those surrounding resource allocation—systematically undermine the best intentions of portfolio management strategy to increase category power. Horizon 2 initiatives are doomed from birth; they will never reach the materiality needed to earn Horizon 1 status.

Here is the key point. This is *not* due to lack of innovation. It is *not* due to weak R&D. It is *not* due to bad product. It is *not* due to lack of customer interest. It is *not* even due to "corporate antibodies," although that gets closer to it.

It is instead due to a complete disconnect between, on the one hand, a field-facing management team driven by a Horizon 1 charter and compensation plan, and on the other, a covey of needy product and market managers with a Horizon 2 set of market development requirements. When these two forces collide, it is no contest: Horizon 1 prevails, hands down. Hence the prevalence of what we have come to call the Horizon 2 gap, a primary symptom of enterprises experiencing Christensen's innovator's dilemma.

Among our clientele, the company that has had the most success in addressing this challenge is Cisco Systems, something we chronicled in both an article (see "To Succeed in the Long Term, Focus on the Middle Term," *Harvard Business*

Review, July–August 2007) and as a case study in *Dealing with Darwin.* With Cisco we developed a set of best practices that they have implemented in relation to their Emerging Technologies Group headed by Marthin De Beer. What follows is an abstraction and generalization of this work into a set of best practices, extended and amended by our work with a number of other clients over the past several years.

CROSSING THE HORIZON 2 CHASM: BEST PRACTICES IN PORTFOLIO MANAGEMENT

There are five areas of management practice that need to be reengineered in order to achieve a balanced portfolio with significant assets in quadrant 2 of the Growth/Materality Matrix. They are:

1. Goals and metrics
2. Planning and budgeting
3. Organization and governance
4. Talent and compensation
5. Mergers and acquisitions

In each case, most practices can remain untouched as they are applied to Horizon 1 and Horizon 3 categories. It is only when a Horizon 2 item is on the agenda that changes must be made. Here's how it all plays out.

Goals and Metrics

As we have already noted, each of the three ROI horizons has a different economic objective. Horizon 1's job is to deliver the forecasted returns in the current fiscal year. By contrast, Horizon 3's job is to deliver next-generation prototypes that portend great things for the future. Thus one might think *flat panel TVs* for Horizon 1 and *3D TVs* for Horizon 3. Horizon 2, in this context, is a kind of ferryboat from the future into the present. Its job is to take a promising next-generation technology and turn it into a material business. Think *Internet-enabled TVs*, for example.

Now in light of the above, it should come as no surprise that success metrics for any one horizon are inappropriate for the other two. This is easily seen when comparing Horizon 1 to Horizon 3, but Horizon 2 often gets lost in the shuffle, never getting its own unique set of metrics. What happens instead is that Horizon 2 efforts initially get measured by Horizon 3 standards, which are too slack, and then after a period of undistinguished performance, they get abruptly re-measured by Horizon 1 metrics, which are too strict. The end result is a whiplash injury that is usually fatal.

A far better way to proceed is to acknowledge the differences among businesses of differing horizons and challenge each to become its best self. Best practice here is illustrated by Figure 2.6.

The goal for Horizon 1 is to run a profitable and sustainable business, and the key performance indicators for so doing should look familiar to all. They are the basis of virtually every annual plan and executive compensation program in publicly held enterprises, and we have nothing new to say about them here.

The metrics for Horizon 3, by contrast, have nothing to do with running a profitable business. They correlate instead with achieving "early market" or "pre-chasm" success, when the goal is simply to put a category on the map. This is done by

Goals, Metrics, and the Three Horizons
Different Metrics for Each Horizon

TIME FRAME	HORIZON 1 (0 – 12 mos)	HORIZON 2 (12 – 36 mos)	HORIZON 3 (36 – 72 mos)
Driving Goal	Maximize Economic Returns	Become a Going Concern	Create a Category
Key Performance Indicators	Revenue vs. plan Bookings Contribution margin Market share Wallet share	Target accts vs. plan Sales velocity Deal size Segment share Time to tipping point	Name–brand customers Deal size Name–brand partners PR buzz Flagship projects
	"Opex"	"Timex"	"Capex"

Figure 2.6

getting one or more name-brand customers to make a major and highly visible commitment to an as-yet-unproven technology. Wal-Mart's commitment to deploy Symbol's RFID for item-level inventory shortly after the tech bust of 2002 is one good example, and the medical group MDVIP's recent commitment to incorporate Navigenics's personal genomic counseling into its concierge-medicine practice is another. Neither creates a sustainable business by itself, but both create the visibility needed to get staged for Horizon 2.

With this as context, we can now turn to Horizon 2 per se. Here the critical goal is to "cross the chasm" between a few flagship customers (Horizon 3) and being a going concern (Horizon 1). The fastest way to do this is by getting at least one niche market to adopt the new Horizon 2 offer as standard. This creates a persistent market for the fledgling effort, championed by a set of deeply committed customers who simply will not let your enterprise off the hook, regardless of how material or not these sales are to its quarterly financial results. That in turn gives the internal leaders of the Horizon 2 effort the clout they need to secure appropriate resources for their next generation of investment. Once a Horizon 2 business has become a going concern, it is no longer a question of whether it will continue to exist but rather to what size it can be scaled.

Looking more closely into this chasm-crossing change in business state, we see that it occurs when prospective customers, who have been interested in making this type of purchase for some time, now regularly see other companies like themselves taking the plunge. They take this as a sign that it is now safe to adopt, and that triggers a tipping point, releasing a flood of engagement. After months and months of sales and marketing efforts trudging uphill and into the wind, suddenly the landscape shifts and you—and your category—are racing downhill with the wind. Customers are now referring prospects to you, and they themselves are signing up for second or third purchases.

Until this tipping point is reached, neither the business nor the category itself can fairly be termed a going concern. Afterward, they both are. So it doesn't take much of a genius to realize that reaching the tipping point is the critical goal for Horizon 2. (Note: the playbook for reaching this state is described in detail in chapter 4.)

The key metrics listed in Figure 2.6 all correlate with tipping-point success. They consist of *quickly* securing significant purchases from a sufficient number of Tier 1 companies within a given target segment, no competitor having comparable success. If we were to turn these into a management-by-objectives plan (MBO), it might look like the following:

> *Secure major sales orders from five to eight of the thirty most influential customers in the target market segment within a twelve- to eighteen-month period, during which no competitor wins more than two.*

Until this metric is met and a tipping point has been achieved, no other metric matters, for the business has not yet become a going concern. Once it is met, then goals and metrics can be transitioned to Horizon 1 standards.

So what's the bit about Opex, Capex, and Timex at the bottom of the table? It's just shorthand for orienting everyone to the scarce resource for each horizon. In the case of Horizon 1, it is operating expense, the goal being to keep the cash cows from drinking up all their own milk. In the case of Horizon 3, it is capital expense, whether that literally comes from the balance sheet or from a "corporate tax" set aside.

In the case of Horizon 2, the scarce resource is time. Experience in the venture community suggests that it can easily take a start-up two to three years to cross a technology-adoption chasm, and that is a close analog to making it through Horizon 2. Unfortunately, experience with public companies says that they cannot wait that long—they have patience for one year, and that can usually be stretched to a second year as long as some progress is visible, but the third year is just too hard to grant. By way of offsetting compensation, established enterprises have strong distribution systems and customer relationships already in place that can, if properly managed, be leveraged by the Horizon 2 team. So the metrics for Horizon 2 are designed to be makeable in four to six quarters, but just barely. There is no room for slack, and every day you do not make visible progress toward closing one or more of your enterprise-validating sales is a bad day.

Planning and Budgeting

The critical best practice here is to subdivide portfolio resource allocation into three separate competitions, one for each horizon, each horizon having its own dedicated pool of resources not to be shared with any of the others. The ROI domains for each horizon are so unique, it makes no sense to have them compete with one another. And if you persist in so doing nonetheless, don't be surprised when Horizon 2 gets the short end. Here's why.

Horizon 1 projects pay off in the current year. Enough said. Horizon 3 projects do not, but they also do not make claims on resources that affect the current year. They are for the future and so keep themselves out of harm's way. But Horizon 2 projects do make claims on resources that affect the present year's results, but they do not pay off in that same year, and that is a *very* tough pill to swallow. No wonder most organizations find some way to spit it out before the planning and budgeting process is done.

Unfortunately, that means nothing gets through Horizon 2. All that wonderful organic innovation for the future that you funded in Horizon 3? All dead on arrival at the shores of Horizon 1. Ditto for any "technology and team" tuck-in acquisitions intended to jump-start your R&D. So if you really are going to behave in this fashion, then shut down all disruptive Horizon 3 projects immediately and direct your money instead solely to incremental improvements in the established lines of business. Why kid yourself?

Alternatively, of course, you can have the hard conversation about just how much present-impacting market-facing resources you are prepared to invest in *any* Horizon 2 effort, and then set aside that pool for Horizon 2 use only. This will vary from year to year, depending on the economy and the current performance of your Horizon 1 portfolio. Once the set-aside is determined, however, all Horizon 2 initiatives must compete with one another to get funded from that pool (and only that pool), but no initiative from any other horizon is allowed to touch it at all. This is earmarking as it was originally intended.

Note that the truly scarce resources are rarely in R&D. Normally they are the field-facing ones: marketing, sales, and services. The critical question then is, what percent of these resources are you willing to dedicate to Horizon 2 efforts only? That is the pool that really matters.

Organization and Governance

Now that we are chartering and resourcing Horizon 2 initiatives appropriately, it is time to organize and govern them appropriately as well. Here the best practices have been illustrated repeatedly by the venture community.

Venture capital gets a lot of credit for Horizon 3 vision, and deservedly so, but its actual returns are more dependent on managing Horizon 2 execution—getting companies and categories across the chasm—and it is Silicon Valley's success rate with this type of effort, not its raw technology innovation, that makes it so hard to replicate. So what are the secrets of its success?

Because virtually all start-ups are funded around a single disruptive innovation, all Horizon 2 initiatives are brought to market by stand-alone, vertically integrated, independent business units with all resources reporting directly to a single, wholly empowered leader—namely, the CEO. This stands in stark contrast to Horizon 2 initiatives in established enterprises, which typically report in to a product manager and are asked to share market-facing resources in sales, marketing, and services with their Horizon 1 counterparts. This sharing creates just enough delay in responsiveness for the venture-backed team to outmaneuver its much larger, better funded, and better known enterprise competition. It is PT boats against aircraft carriers, and in the narrow waters of the chasm, it is no contest.

But large enterprises simply cannot afford to spin up independent business units every time they have a Horizon 2 initiative—or can they? Well, what really must be kept off the table is generating a host of business units at scale, each with a full complement of staff in every line function. That generates an overhead structure that is madness. But it is possible is to create *temporary, virtually integrated business units*, which is all you really need. Here's how you do it.

First, identify a genuinely entrepreneurial leader who will be the virtual GM of the unit for the entirety of the Horizon 2 effort, all eight quarters. Charter this as a do-or-die, "burn the boats" affair. Then allow that GM to recruit resources to the team from each of the line functions. These people will not actually be transferred out of their current organizations, but their fully burdened costs will be reallocated to the Horizon 2 initiative, and for the duration of their involvement in it, they will take all their direction from the virtual GM. Performance and salary reviews are still done within the line organizations, so careers are not derailed, but they are understandably highly influenced by the input of the virtual GM. Finally, when the Horizon 2 initiative is over, these same people either go back to their host organizations, carrying with them invaluable expertise in a new line of business that is now ready to be integrated into the line functions, or they move on to the next Horizon 2 project, carrying a bunch of best practices with them.

This approach allows established enterprises to field agile organizations that can compete effectively against dedicated start-ups while avoiding the kind of empire building that a purely vertical structure all too often entails. At the same time, virtual business units are natural units of governance by which executive management and the board can retain direct line of sight into Horizon 2 performance.

Finally, because they are so high risk and time sensitive, Horizon 2 initiatives should be executing to a rapid-fire, highly transparent cadence of weekly commits, monthly reviews, and quarterly milestones. The weekly commits are with the virtual GM, the monthly reviews with executive management, and the quarterly milestones with the board of directors.

That's pretty much how venture capital does it. And there is no reason why you can't too. It's just that, unlike venture capital, given all your Horizon 1 commitments, you cannot do very many of these. Therefore it is critical that the few you can do, you do right.

Talent and Compensation

If organization is where established enterprises do want to emulate venture capital, talent and compensation is where they do not. The venture model pushes much harder at the frontier of the possible, takes greater risk for greater reward, and can afford to back entrepreneurs who "break a lot of glass." Established enterprises are not well served by any of these approaches.

Instead, the focus should be on recruiting entrepreneurial leaders from the pool of high-potential managers just below the executive ranks, offering them a chance to showcase their talents in a high-visibility, highly challenging assignment. In so doing, they should have strong mentors who can help them recruit effectively, attack the market forcefully, and work around internal obstacles gracefully. And everyone else on the team should be getting a version of this same experience appropriate to their level and assignment.

Now, because this path is not the norm, you will often find you have recruited the wrong people for some portion of the jobs at hand. No harm, no foul—that is to be expected. What the virtual GM cannot do is delay replacing them even for an instant. No probationary period, no 90-day improvement programs, none of that—there simply isn't time. Instead, one must be able to turn them back over to their line function with no consequences to their personnel file and with an added quarter of fully loaded expense coverage to make up for the disruption caused. Then choose more wisely next time.

Finally, on the compensation side, no need to try to emulate the stock-option returns that power venture-backed start-up teams to work late into the night. If people want that sort of compensation, send them to Mohr Davidow Ventures on Sand Hill Road in Menlo Park (where, full disclosure, I am a venture partner). People inside established enterprises are not taking start-up risk. Moreover, although the Horizon-1-oriented organization can be an obstacle, it can also be an asset if managed carefully. It is certainly easier to get access to a hot prospect with Cisco written on your business card rather than Apitaxis, or whatever other weird word you could acquire the URL for when it came time to name your company.

What compensation should do, on the other hand, is focus the team intensely and exclusively on achieving its key goals and metrics. This is particularly important for sales compensation. Horizon 2 is not about revenue maximization. It is about key account wins in a specific target segment. So you need to tweak the sales compensation to tie it primarily to this outcome and allow the same metric to put a strong tilt to everyone else's bonus as well.

Mergers and Acquisitions

Most M&A transactions are not for Horizon 2 but rather serve as alternatives to it. One class is Horizon 1 consolidations in mature categories, along the lines of what Oracle is doing in this decade and what Computer Associates was famous for in a past one. This is a growth engine that does not rely on category growth at all. At the other end of the spectrum, there are financially immaterial acquisitions of next-generation technologies in Horizon 3, used to kick start R&D in a category that looks promising but has yet to truly emerge. These are the seeds of future Horizon 2 bets.

In contrast to these, Horizon 2 acquisitions should be specifically intended to get the enterprise into a Stage B high-growth category that it either missed or whiffed. Cisco managed such a recovery very successfully in the 1990s when it acquired three companies in the LAN switching category—Kalpana, Granite, and Grand Junction—thereby entering a hot category and protecting its router franchise from erosion from below. BEA did the same when it acquired WebLogic (to get into Web application servers), as did EMC with VMware (virtualization software), and Adobe with Macromedia (streaming media).

The key to success with Horizon 2 M&A is to acquire companies with revenues that make them material to your financials from the outset. It is hard enough to navigate the internal resource-allocation dynamics of Horizon 2 with an organic innovation championed by people everyone knows. It is virtually impossible to do so with an acquisition led by a team of strangers. They simply have not had time to earn the necessary credibility with their colleagues to gain their support, nor do they know enough about where the bodies are buried to avoid being saddled with cast-off resources.

Instead, think of successful Horizon 2 acquisitions as Horizon 1 companies in their stand-alone state that become Horizon 2 in the context of your larger ambitions. This is the spirit in which Intel has recently acquired McAfee, a stand-alone PC security company, to help it get into mobile devices, new territory for both companies. And when Cisco acquired Linksys, a stand-alone consumer router company, it did so in part to create economically viable endpoints for an end-to-end service provider architecture for home entertainment. Similarly, its acquisition of Webex, an established player in small to medium business Web conferencing, gives it a leg up in expanding the enterprise market for communication and collaboration technologies.

One final note: a sticking point for following this strategy is usually acquisition price. Established enterprises hate paying higher multiples for their acquisitions than they can earn for themselves. But the truth is, pure-play Stage B growth companies do deserve a higher price-to-earnings multiple than a mixed portfolio, so as the gangsters say in the movies, don't take it personally. The good news for executives in the present era is that many established enterprises are so flush with cash, there has rarely been an easier time to bite this bullet.

On the other hand, if you persist in faltering at Horizon 2, eventually your Horizon 1 portfolio will fall out of favor, and your stock price will fall below a level at which it can be used for acquisition currency. Then, unless you have a big balance sheet, you are in dire straits indeed. There is no path forward that maintains your independence, and your best bet may be to merge with a competitor or suffer the slings and arrows of the private-equity buyout community. Neither bodes well for your career, but both at least preserve some of the jobs people were hoping you would be creating a future for.

WRAPPING UP

Category Power is the most powerful tool in the toolbox for creating escape velocity. Used to advantage, it continually repositions your company for attractive growth opportunities and steers it clear of sinkholes. But experience has shown that most enterprises falter in this critical effort, and this chapter has attempted to show why and what can be done about it.

To close out our discussion, we're going to take a deeper look into a single case example, that of Akamai, where (full disclosure) I have been a board member since 2006, and how it leveraged category power to realign its portfolio for higher margins and greater stability.

Case Example: Managing the Category Portfolio at Akamai—2006 to 2010

Akamai Technologies runs a network atop the Internet leveraging more than 73,000 servers in nearly a thousand networks in more than seventy countries. On any given day, this metanetwork carries between 20 and 30 percent of the total worldwide Web traffic. Its value add is that it can intelligently and dynamically route and reroute traffic in order to minimize the delay in getting from point A to point B over the public Internet.

In 2006 the company had two primary offers—a content-delivery network, or CDN, optimized for downloading static content, be that streaming media or large software files, and a technology platform called EdgeSuite, optimized for dynamic content, used to accelerate a variety of interactive applications. The company was best known for its CDN, and it was hard for the EdgeSuite applications to break away from the gravitational field of the core business. This was particularly concerning because management felt the CDN business was being increasingly exposed to commoditization and that the future of the company needed to be anchored by value-added services.

As a result, management launched a pair of initiatives that brought all three ROI horizons into play. The first of these involved reorganizing the customer-facing functions around five vertical categories, as follows:

- **Media and Entertainment**, where the interest in CDN was strongest, particularly around streaming media.
- **High Tech**, where there was also ongoing strong demand for CDN for the purpose of managing software downloads, as well as growing demand for accelerating online applications.
- **Retail Commerce**, where the big concern was response time on consumer-facing sites, where delays could lead prospects to leave the site or abandon their shopping carts midtransaction.

- **Enterprise**, where the interest was in running interactive enterprise IT applications, like sales force automation or business intelligence, on mobile client devices or in remote locations.
- **Public Sector**, where bespoke projects led by professional services are the norm, whether for specialized applications or e-government initiatives.

In conjunction with this reshaping of the customer-facing functions, a companion set of initiatives redesigned Akamai's portfolio of offerings to better align it with these vertical categories. This played out as follows:

- **The CDN offer set**, a Horizon 1 business, already matched up well with Media and Entertainment and High Tech and was the least affected by the changes. Now everyone who sold CDN to the entertainment industry was a media expert, a skill set somewhat akin to dancing with elephants. The result of having such focused expertise in the field has been more-productive relationships with huge media buyers, something critical to Akamai's business success.
- A new business, born of EdgeSuite technology, called **Dynamic Site Acceleration** or DSA, focused on the challenges of retail commerce. Management had anticipated this would be a Horizon 2 business, but in fact the new offer was close enough to the prior EdgeSuite offer, and the value proposition was so immediate and compelling, that it turned out to be Horizon 1 almost from birth. There simply was not much of a chasm to cross.
- Another new business, also born of EdgeSuite technology, called **Web Application Acceleration** or WAA,

focused on the challenges enterprise IT CIOs face in supporting remote mobile applications over the public Internet. This did turn out to be a Horizon 2 business, about which more later.

- A third new business, based on novel technology, called **Advertising Decision Services** or ADS, focused on the concerns of advertisers to get better yields from their Web-based campaigns. This was a new market and a new offer set, so management organized it as a Horizon 3 initiative, which it has proved to be, only in the current year beginning to stage itself for transition to Horizon 2, some two years after initial funding.

Returning to the Horizon 2 challenge faced specifically by Web Application Acceleration, first let me note that it has been met handily. Although Akamai does not break out its revenue reporting in this category, in the 2010 fiscal year, the business enjoyed substantial revenue growth. Moreover, combined with its sister offer in DSA, the two value-added businesses surpassed the core CDN business in terms of total contribution to revenues and earnings. As a result, the future of Akamai is now firmly anchored on top of a value-adding, commoditization-resistant foundation as a complement to its ongoing strongly performing CDN business.

So how did the company bring this off? Some of the key elements include the following:

- **Mapping the WAA initiative specifically to the enterprise IT sales channel.** While this did not give the business a dedicated sales channel, it did give it top of mind in the field and did so while avoiding the high overhead of an overlay sales force. Moreover, it kept the WAA team from diluting its efforts in other segments where the demand for its offer was subordinate to others in the Akamai portfolio. (Early on in the WAA effort, Akamai did fund a completely separate channel. It found, however, that it was more expensive and less effective than aligning it with a vertical sales channel whose customers put a high value on application performance over the Web.)

- **Acquiring another company in the space.** In 2007 Akamai acquired Netli, a company focused exclusively on the Web application acceleration category. At the time, both operations had around $10 million in revenue, so in addition to adding technology and management depth, this gave the fledgling WAA business a kick start toward materiality.

- **Hitting upon a great virtual GM.** Akamai was fortunate in that an executive who came in with the Netli acquisition, Willie Tejada, had the kind of customer-facing scrappy entrepreneurial attitude that Horizon 2 initiatives need. While at Netli, he had competed with Akamai and had great respect for the company's strengths and was both eager and able to mobilize them to accelerate the transition to materiality. He reported to a longtime senior Akamai executive, Chris Schoettle, who sponsored the acquisition and helped him navigate the inevitable internal obstacles to any new business gaining escape velocity.

- **Reporting out regularly to the board of directors.** This gave the Horizon 2 initiative the kind of visibility and management attention needed to encourage its escape velocity. In particular, field sales got the kind of encouragement needed to go the extra mile on its behalf.

- **Catching the wave for cloud computing.** As
software-as-a-service and cloud computing have become more and more important to enterprise IT strategies, the demand for accelerating applications running
over the public Internet is shooting up. Akamai's investment in organic innovation, complemented with a timely "tuck in" acquisition, is proving prescient.

The overall lesson of Akamai, at least from this board
member's perspective, is that solving for the Horizon 2 gap
is not all that hard once everyone is aligned to the program.
The introduction of a third set of success metrics specific to
the horizon was particularly key for a culture like Akamai's,
where accountability looms large. By making sure it was
being accountable to the right things, this management team
was able to succeed in achieving escape velocity from the
pull of its legacy business model.

CHAPTER THREE

Company Power: Making Asymmetrical Bets

C ompany power is the sum of all the bargaining power you can bring to bear relative to your customers, your suppliers, your sales-channel partners, and your whole-offer partners. In this context, HP under Mark Hurd dramatically increased its bargaining power, in large part by squeezing its existing businesses in order to generate returns and stock price appreciation that let it buy up additional businesses, leveraging the increase in bulk purchasing power to get better deals from suppliers, more coverage from sales-channel partners, and a bigger footprint to motivate whole-offer partners. All that bargaining power was a function of HP's differentiation relative to its competitive set (IBM and Oracle) and relative to what each of the constituencies above values most—in HP's case, reliable although not particularly differentiated products and services at a significantly lower price.

This is a classic operational excellence strategy for increasing company power, the sort of thing we have seen from Southwest Airlines and Wal-Mart, but not commonly from a Tier 1 enterprise IT company. It was certainly not something that IBM or Oracle was likely to copy. And that is the key to increasing company power.

Achieving escape velocity means freeing yourself from power-deflating bake-offs with competing companies by creating one or more unmatchable offers. The path to such an outcome is illustrated by Figure 3.1.

The diagram illustrates a number of claims, each of which is critical to creating and executing a company-power strategy:

- Your company is a member of a competitive set, one that consists of you and every other company that customers and partners perceive to offer comparable, and therefore potentially substitutable, offers.
- The availability of these potential substitutes mitigates your bargaining power with customers and partners. This makes your offers harder to sell and puts revenues and profit margins under pressure.
- At the same time, however, the existence of a viable competitive set reassures customers and partners that worthwhile value is being created and that there are backup alternatives in case any given offer or vendor falls short of the mark. This makes your offers easier to buy.
- The large asterisk sitting outside the circle denotes that it is possible for one company—specifically, your

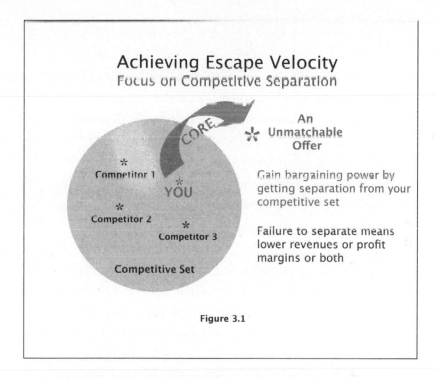

Achieving Escape Velocity
Focus on Competitive Separation

CORE

An Unmatchable Offer

Gain bargaining power by getting separation from your competitive set

Failure to separate means lower revenues or profit margins or both

Competitor 1

YOU

Competitor 2

Competitor 3

Competitive Set

Figure 3.1

company—to develop a capability that, at least for some appreciable amount of time, can generate offers unmatchable by the competitive set.

- The absence of viable substitutes increases your company's bargaining power, making your offers easier to sell, thereby improving your revenues and profits. At the same time, because you continue to be affiliated with an established category, they also remain easy to buy. Customers are delighted and engaged; partners, on the other hand, are feeling challenged by your newfound clout. This is the optimal position for making money and maximizing returns to your shareholders.

- The arrow that leads from your current state to this highly desirable future state represents the investment and innovation required to achieve this success.

The greater the force embodied in this arrow, i.e., the further from reach your novel capability is able to establish itself, the less likely that competitors will succeed—or even try—to neutralize its unique value.

- This vector of investment and innovation is your *core*. It is what makes you different and sets you apart from your competitive set. (*Context*, by contrast, is everything else you invest in to make yourself the same in order to be part of that competitive set.)

Being laser-focused about the specific direction of your core innovation investments and being Star-Trek-bold about skewing resource allocation to their specific ends together let you achieve escape velocity from your category norms. Unfortunately, most companies fall short on both counts. As a result, they live within the confines of their competitive set most of the time. Can Chrysler really set itself apart from General Motors? Can United Airlines truly differentiate from American Airlines? Is it that much better to go public with Goldman Sachs than with Morgan Stanley or Credit Suisse? Is GEICO really cheaper than State Farm? Does it have to be Pepsi—can't it be Coke (or vice versa)? Most of the time, either one is OK, really.

But not always. Sometimes there really is no acceptable substitute. And when companies do succeed in setting themselves distinctively apart, when they do escape the gravitational field of their competitive sets, the results can be pretty spectacular, as they have been for Prius, Amazon, Apple, Google, Facebook, Cisco, and IBM. On the other hand, when they do not succeed in actually separating, it is by no means a disaster. There's just a lot more hard work to be done to earn a much smaller reward. Ask the folks who have worked at Nissan, Borders, Palm, AskJeeves, Friendster, 3Com, or Unisys.

So what is the difference? After all, every company has a strategy to be different, and all invest heavily in R&D and marketing and operations. What ingredient is present in the few that actually do get to escape velocity? The answer, I submit, is *leadership.*

Now it is fashionable to believe that leaders are to be found at the top of every Fortune 500 company, but in reality the kind of leadership we are talking about here is relatively rare. It requires committing to choices that everyone else in your competitive set eschews. *How smart can that be?* It requires skewing resource allocation, sometimes radically, never without consternation, often over the objections of not only members of your own management team but longtime customers and partners as well. *Is that really wise?* It requires being willing to be wrong, sometimes dramatically and always publicly. *Are you really up for that?* And finally, it requires the authentic enlistment and sustained engagement of the entire management team along with the board of directors. *When was the last time you got that?*

Nonetheless, without this kind of breakaway leadership, there is no way to achieve escape velocity. So, wise as it may be to steer the middle course, know that it will likely bind you forever to your competitive set, allowing both customers and partners to play all of you off against one another in a perpetual effort to reduce your price and margins. Some on your team may actually be OK with this outcome, but your investors are not likely to share that view, and if they exit and the bottom-feeders come in, then you and all around you will feel the chill hand of "rationalization" and "reengineering" steering the company to a future in which you personally are not likely to play a part.

In this context, the path to escape velocity doesn't seem so dangerous after all. And the truth is, it is not. But it does require you and your colleagues to align precisely around three key elements:

1. **Your competitive set.** The more precise you can be about which companies you are genuinely competing with and why, the smaller you can make the circle of competition from which you need to escape and the more likely you will be to actually escape it. The question to ask: different *from whom?*

2. **Your core differentiation.** The more precise you can be about the specific investment and innovation required to develop the unmatchable capabilities that lead to escape velocity, the more traction you will get, and the less waste you will create. The question to ask: different *in what way?*

3. **Your execution strategy.** The more precise you can be about the puts and takes needed to fund and staff your investment and innovation commitments, both in the factory and in the field, the less internal friction you create and the more alignment you enable. The question to ask: different *by what means?*

Getting clarity and precision around these three elements, then acting in accordance with the dictates you declare, will create company power—period. No magic is required. That said, there are subtleties to understand and pitfalls to avoid, and the rest of this chapter is devoted to instructing you in both before setting you on your way.

YOUR COMPETITIVE SET— DIFFERENT FROM WHOM?

Who exactly is in your competitive set, really? For years Scott McNealy, CEO of Sun, routinely made fun of Microsoft, contrasting it to Sun, often in very amusing if cynical ways. It made for great theater. The problem was, Microsoft was not in Sun's competitive set—not then, not now, not ever. So this made for very expensive theater indeed.

Ask yourself, is Kia part of BMW's competitive set? Does Wal-Mart compete with Neiman Marcus? How do you know? More important, when it comes to your company, how do you decide?

When focusing on competition, it helps to clear your mind first, for it is likely to be clogged with defensive, self-centered explanations about why your offers are better than theirs. Rest assured, on this score, nobody cares what you think. Here are some things people do care about:

- Where there is no competition, there is no market. This is why start-ups who "have no competition" have trouble engaging partners and making sales. Your competitive set is part of your overall value proposition. So choose it with care.
- You are judged by the company you keep. If you persist in talking down your competition, people will conclude you hang out with riffraff, and that will reflect on you. By contrast, if you position yourself credibly relative to worthy alternatives, that speaks well on your behalf. Dissing and differentiating are two very different activities.

- Your competitive set is the primary means by which customers and partners understand your role in the marketplace. By claiming that you can substitute for these companies, at least under certain conditions, you give them a basis for evaluating your offers. So be ambitious, but be real.
- Finally, your competitive set provides the context for understanding and valuing your differentiation, which provides a basis for tilting a purchase decision your way.

If you can put yourself in the shoes of a customer or a partner, you can construct a competitive set that will help you become more powerful even as it helps them become more successful. But you have to work within the limits of their interest in you. This calls for some pretty radical simplification, which can be achieved by paring down the field of competition in two generic ways. The first is to compete within your own *business architecture*; the second, to compete within your own *tier*. Here's how each plays out.

Business architecture is an idea that seems a bit abstract at first but turns out to be easy to understand in practice and surprisingly powerful. It is anchored in the observation that large successful enterprises consolidate around two—and only two—fundamental approaches to creating value, as illustrated in Figure 3.2.

1. The **Complex Systems** business architecture specializes in highly customized solutions to very complex challenges. Its customer lists range from government programs, of which there are typically only a few, to enterprises, of which there might be hundreds, to small businesses, of which there might be thousands. But its

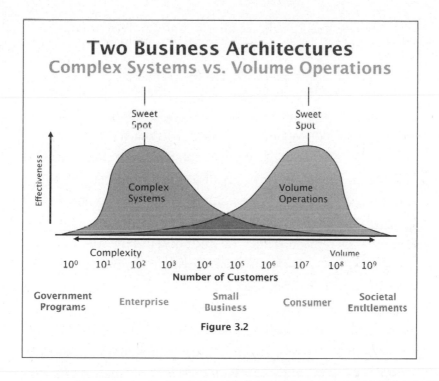

Two Business Architectures
Complex Systems vs. Volume Operations

Figure 3.2

sweet spot is the enterprise space where it makes millions of dollars from each of hundreds of customers. Cisco, IBM, SAP, Accenture, and Oracle are all predominantly complex systems companies in this context.

2. The **Volume Operations** business architecture specializes in highly packaged products or service transactions that address everyday needs for large masses of people. This can range from societal entitlements that touch hundreds of millions of citizens to consumer products and services that touch tens of millions to highly standardized offers that support tens of thousands of home and small businesses. Its sweet spot is the consumer market, where it makes tens of dollars per purchase from millions of consumers on a weekly or monthly basis. Apple, Nokia, Facebook, Zynga, Sony,

Twitter, and Google are all predominantly volume operations companies.

We have written at length about these two architectures, both in the *Harvard Business Review* ("Strategy and Your Stronger Hand," December 2005) and in *Dealing with Darwin*, chapter 3. The essence of this material is that all markets self-organize around this pair of architectures, supporting a different market leader for each, the expectation being that over time the volume operations offers will encroach on the complex systems territory, eventually forcing the complex systems offers to evolve to a new level of complexity, thereby opening up the next market frontier.

In order to focus company power by restricting your competitive set, it is enough to know that customers almost never make purchase comparisons across the boundary between complex systems and volume operations. At the margin, they either want to pay up for the customization of the former or save money via the standardization of the latter. Thus if you are a large business looking for an information system, you will look to SAP or Oracle, not to Intuit or Microsoft. If you are a small business looking for computer power, you will be thinking about a PC or a Mac, not HP Linux servers or EMC storage. Small businesses have no desire to be called on by an IBM sales rep, and large businesses have no use for half-off coupons redeemable at Frys.

Your company may not be operating at either of these extremes, but at the end of the day, customers and partners need to know which of these two architectures you are ultimately committed to. The first is primarily a systems and projects affair; the second, products and transactions: which one better reflects your intent?

Whichever you choose, the clearest way to express your decision is by the companies you include in your competitive set. That is why we were so critical of Sun, a complex-systems company, calling out Microsoft, a volume-operations company, as a reference competitor. To be sure, Microsoft has systematically encroached on all Sun's markets, but Sun's demise was due not to that but rather to its inability to evolve to the next level of complexity. It got caught out in a no-man's land between Microsoft and Intel coming up from the bottom, and IBM and HP coming down from the top, hoping near the end to find a third alternative business architecture in cloud computing, but not succeeding (in part validating our belief that no such third architecture exists). So it is not just customers and partners you can confuse by being muddy on this issue—it is your own employees as well.

Once you've privileged one architecture over the other, the second dimension of your competitive space to restrict through focus is which *tier* in the market you are competing in. This works something like flights in a golf tournament or ratings in amateur tennis. In the case of markets, it self-organizes into three tiers, as follows:

- **Tier 1: The market leaders at the top of the heap.** Think United Airlines, American Airlines, or Southwest Airlines. Think Toyota, General Motors, or Daimler AG.
- **Tier 2: The other brand-name players in the game.** Think Delta Airlines, Alaska Airlines, or US Airways. Think Honda, Nissan, or Audi.
- **Tier 3: The remaining, largely unheralded, players in the category.** Think Aloha Airlines, Air Nevada, or Freedom Air. Think Suzuki, Isuzu, or Kia.

The key point to make here is that selling partners, solution partners, suppliers, and customers self-select to focus on one of these three tiers and largely ignore the other two. Classically, Tier 1 attracts customers looking for the *safe buy* and willing to pay up for it, whereas Tier 3 attracts those who see the category as a commodity and are looking for the *lowest price*, and Tier 2 attracts those looking for something out of the ordinary, specific to their particular needs or taste, what one might call the *thinking person's choice*.

While these sets may overlap at their boundaries, at their center points they are separate and distinct and do not invite comparison. That means, at any given time, while you may be indirectly competing with companies in another tier, you are directly competing only with the companies in your own. Even if you have ambitions to move up a tier, you must first create definitive competitive separation from other companies in your current tier in order to escape that tier's gravitational field.

Now, by the time you have aligned with one of the two architectures and one of the three tiers, you have potentially achieved a six-to-one reduction in your competitive set, paring it down to the companies that people really do compare you to and you really do intend to substitute for. In this context, there is typically one company that looms as the obvious alternative to you. That company is your *reference competitor* by default. You may choose to embrace this pairing or to reposition yourself in relation to an alternative reference competitor, and this choice determines the core of your *positioning strategy*.

A reference competitor provides the foil against which you will demonstrate your strategic differentiation. Let me give a simple example from a bygone era. In the days of minicomputers and mainframes and supercomputers, a company called Convex was launching a product with dramatic new price-performance appeal. It had to make a decision as to whether to position this product as a super-minicomputer or a mini-supercomputer, and it turned out the difference between the two was profound. If it chose the former, its reference competitor would be DEC, the leader in minicomputers at the time, and its challenge would be staying ahead in R&D. If it chose the latter, its reference competitor would be Cray, the leader in supercomputing, and its challenge would be in finding big enough markets to support its growth. You can see what a difference this makes. Which partners do you most want to attract? Which customers? Which subcategory offers you the best future prospects? This is the stuff of positioning strategy. (FYI, Convex chose the latter strategy, rode it well across the chasm, got stuck in the bowling alley gutter, and was eventually acquired by HP in 1995—isn't Wikipedia wonderful?)

Here are some more-contemporary examples. In each case, a company is targeting a reference competitor who is a worthy alternative for some applications but who serves as the perfect foil to highlight the company's strategic positioning of its escape-velocity core:

- **Cognizant**, the fastest-growing global services provider over the past decade, originally chose Infosys, the leading Indian company in the category, as its reference competitor, seeking to share a common reputation for technology innovation and to differentiate based on adaptability to the customer. However, now that its revenues are fast approaching Infosys's, the company has decided to shift its reference competitor to Accenture, signaling an intent to migrate to the highest tier in this market. Here it expects to differentiate on innovation and thought leadership, repositioning itself as a company to bring to the table much earlier in the business dialogue.

- **MySpace** and **hi5**, the number-two and number-three players in social networks, have both been forced to reposition themselves in the wake of Facebook's global dominance of the category. There is simply no room for a second social network. MySpace, therefore, is refocusing on entertainment, specifically music, although it has yet to call out a reference competitor. And hi5 is moving into social gaming, where its reference competitor will be Zynga by default. Again, reference competitors help everyone in the ecosystem know what your company is up to, something that is particularly important when you are changing course.

- During the tech boom, **Dell** benefited from having first Compaq and then HP as its reference competitors, being able to share in their brand reputations for quality and reliability and being able to showcase its differentiated business model. In the past decade, however, as the industry consolidated, HP became a PC-centric reference competitor, and Dell became perceived as being stuck in a commoditizing volume-operations category. Thus in the past few years, the company has been repositioning itself to accentuate a complex-systems capability, in no small part by buying Perot Systems, and is now positioning against the complex-systems, enterprise side of the HP house. No more Dell dudes; now more Dell does.

- When Carol Bartz took over the CEO role at **Yahoo!**, the company was trapped in a reference competition with Google that it simply could not win. By selling off the search business to Microsoft, she was able to break this comparison and refocus the company on its media capabilities. Here her challenge is that the digital media landscape is so fragmented that Yahoo! has no direct reference competitor of merit, although Facebook may well end up filling that role, allowing Yahoo! to showcase its media aggregation assets as its core differentiation.

To sum up, we began our discussion of competitive sets with the intent of simplifying the context for communicating our strategic differentiation. But there is an additional benefit as well: it is much easier to escape the gravitational field of a tightly defined category, ideally symbolized by a single reference competitor, than to break free from a cloud of competitors who, taken collectively, can be all over the map.

Your reference competitor represents the *from* in a *from-to arc* that describes the journey of differentiation you are embarked upon. The clearer you can be about your point of embarkation, the better. Then you need to pair this *from* with a *to*, a point of arrival. What is going to be your claim to fame, the foundation of your unmatchable offer? To answer that question, you must declare your core.

DECLARING YOUR CORE—DIFFERENT IN WHAT WAY?

You want to differentiate dramatically and sustainably in order to increase your bargaining power with customers and partners so as to achieve higher revenues and greater profits.

Well and good. But why would the world cooperate in helping you achieve this end, given that it will end up paying more for your offers than it does today? Normally the world is looking for cheaper, faster, better, and that goal is achieved by keeping you inside the bounds of a substitutable competitive set. Given that you want to do the opposite, how can you get the world on your side?

Well, it turns out the world does not *always* want cheaper, faster, better. That is what it wants as long as the category stays on its current trajectory. As long as PCs are going to be overly complex and highly demanding, I am going to want a cheaper, faster, better PC. But that is not what I *really* want. I really want the category to trend in a different direction altogether, as does the world, as demonstrated by its hyperenthusiastic embrace of the Apple iPad. It is a question of what you are going to put your core in service to—the status quo, in which case you must deliver better, faster, cheaper and there is little more to say about the subject, or a new trajectory, in which case you have a blank canvas upon which to paint, which does require some further commentary.

New trajectories are created by unmatchable capabilities that produce novel offerings that prove irresistible to customers. These offers are anchored in unique core competencies, as the examples in Figure 3.3 illustrate.

COMPANY	CORE CAPABILITY	REPRESENTATIVE OFFERING
Apple	User experience design	iPhone
IBM	Technical R&D	Watson
Google	Rapid innovation	Android
Oracle	Mature market M&A	Consolidated ERP
Amazon	Disruptive innovation	Elastic cloud computing
Pixar	Animated story-telling	*Toy Story*

Figure 3.3

Each of these companies has dramatically distanced themselves from their competitive set, and by so doing has changed the very buying criteria by which customers evaluate their category.

When you undertake such an ambitious agenda, your core becomes the fulcrum upon which the category pivots. In other words, because of a unique capability that only you can provide, the category will evolve in a better way, one so deeply satisfying to the customers and partners you are targeting that they will do whatever they can to further your success. Now what in the world could be so powerful as to enable you to do that? Your *crown jewels.*

Crown jewels are enterprise capabilities that are valuable, defensible, and unique to your company and that, if developed and accentuated properly, create sustainable competitive advantages that enable distinctive competitive separation. The jewels metaphor is deliberately "loose" because our experience has been that these capabilities can be quite varied in nature, but here are some of the more common types:

- **Technology.** These jewels are almost always patented to ensure defensibility; they include Google's search algorithms, HP's inkjet printing, Cisco's Internet Operating System, as well as the molecular makeup of every pharmaceutical on patent.
- **Expertise.** These jewels are not patentable but are both scarce and hard to acquire, often meeting the definition of trade secrets. They include the more confidential elements of Apple's design expertise, Intel's semiconductor process expertise, and SAP's business process expertise, as well as Accenture's customer domain expertise needed to focus vertical market offers effectively.
- **Platform products.** These are products from your company that you have made available to other vendors in your industry for the purpose of deploying their own offerings. When a company owns a proprietary platform product, it has enormous company power, like Microsoft with Windows, Oracle with the Oracle relational database, and Qualcomm with its CDMA technology.
- **A passionate customer base.** This is what kept Apple in the game through all the lean years and made the Grateful Dead one of the most reliable draws in entertainment history. It was what Tiger Woods lost in 2010, not coincidentally along with a huge chunk of his net worth.
- **Scale.** Being the biggest usually means you can be the baddest, especially when it comes to negotiating with suppliers and beating competitors on price. Wal-Mart is a long-time jewel holder here, and HP, currently the world's largest computer company, is a newer entrant.
- **Brand.** In consumer markets in particular, where

the noise of promotions can drown out even the best funded marketing messages, having a recognized brand is a huge advantage, even when it needs refurbishing. Thus there is persistent value in brands like AT&T, Budweiser, Flickr, and YouTube even after they have all changed hands.

- **Business model.** When the world is stuck in the old way, a new way can have dramatic impact. Look at what FedEx did to package delivery, Southwest Airlines did to air travel, and more recently, what Salesforce .com is doing to enterprise software and what Mozilla is doing with browsers.

What are *your* crown jewels? Do you have any at all? Are they powerful enough to fulfill your company-power ambitions? Could they become so if you invested in them more deeply? These are questions that executive teams must answer collectively and unanimously in order to achieve escape velocity. The idea is not complicated, and the questions are not deceptive, but dealing with the anxieties and insecurities that they surface can be both. Nonetheless, you must get through them. Company-power strategy starts here.

Specifically, it is precisely at the intersection of what the world wants you to be and what your crown jewels can enable you to become, right where an emerging mission-critical need meets a heretofore unavailable capability, that your company's *core* wants to lie. Core is the essence of company power. It is that which sets the direction of your escape trajectory. It is where you need to lead first, committing yourself to a performance that is extravagantly differentiated, and then manage second, figuring out how in the world you are going to pay for all this and still stay out of jail.

Let's consider some current examples of companies looking to leverage their crown jewels to alter the trajectory of an established category, to the delight of their target customers and partners:

- **Adobe.** Computer-enabled self-service systems today are ubiquitous and becoming more so, but that does not keep them from being confusing, irritating, and unattractive. Adobe is taking its crown jewels in user experience design, rich Internet application development tools, and enterprise workflow, and putting them all in service to a new trajectory, one designed to help its enterprise customers delight their consumers rather than confound them, what the company is calling Customer Engagement Management.
- **Cisco.** Digital communications are proliferating like crazy, but in disconnected silos—desk phone, cell phone, text, IM, e-mail, voicemail, Web conferencing, video conferencing. What we want is for all these facilities to interoperate seamlessly—but that is not the trajectory the industry is currently on. Cisco is taking its crown jewel—the network as a platform—and putting it in service to Unified Communications under a Collaboration Architecture.
- **Compuware.** Because Internet applications grew up many decades after data center applications were established, the two are bolted together somewhat awkwardly, and while each domain has many tools to support it, the people responsible for managing application performance cannot readily monitor things end to end. Compuware is taking its two crown jewels, Gomez, a leading Internet monitor, with Vantage, a leading data

center monitor, and welding them together to create just such an end-to-end application management platform.

These are all examples of how companies are taking advantage of crown jewels by using them to achieve escape velocity. However, they do not answer the question of how to develop the crown jewel in the first place. This requires executive teams to make highly asymmetrical bets, a topic to which we shall now turn.

COMPANY POWER THROUGH ASYMMETRICAL BETS—*DIFFERENT BY WHAT MEANS?*

To make a difference of the magnitude we have been describing—to bring that difference into existence and instantiate it in your company—calls for an approach we term *Lead first, manage second.*

Lead first means committing to a deeply asymmetrical bet on core before you allow yourself to become enmeshed in last year's operating plan. There are a number of best practices associated with this approach, as follows:

1. **Secure buy-in at the top before you launch.** Let's be clear: when it comes to making asymmetrical bets, there can be no bystanders in the game, no nonrowing passengers in the boat. If someone just cannot get behind the commitment, he or she has to be replaced, and by far the best time to do that, for everyone involved, is right at the beginning.
2. **Publish the vision and the road map.** This is how you declare core. The vision is not about you, it is about

the new trajectory for the category, the one that will delight customers, attract partners, and inspire employees. The road map, on the other hand, is about you. It highlights the game-changing offers you intend to deliver by the grace of your crown jewels and an asymmetrical bet to capitalize upon them.

3. **Burn the boats.** Take the option of retreat off the table. Yes, there is a Plan B for the company but not for the current leadership team. If we fail, we all expect to be fired. Or as the ancient Greeks used to say, we will come home with our shields or on them.

4. **Fund core first.** Keep this effort outboard of managing business as usual by committing to it in advance. Give it precedence over everything else, and continually revisit its needs to ensure you are gaining the necessary competitive separation. For practical purposes, this means there is not one ops review, there are two—one for core and one for everything else—and they should not be mixed.

5. **Use "whatever it takes" as your funding and staffing standard.** The last thing you want to do is come up short on core. If you fail to gain escape velocity, you will not only have wasted an enormous amount of resources but will have incurred a huge opportunity cost as well. So once you are in, go all in. Make absolutely sure you give your core effort everything you have got. The most dangerous thing you can do is "play safe."

6. **Commit to major-market tipping points as your metric of success.** The company is doing everything in its power to make this effort a success. The leaders in charge of the effort are accountable for returning a

home run. Singles and doubles don't cut it—you have to hit the ball out of the park. This means nothing less than changing the buying criteria for the category as a whole.

Steve Jobs gets tremendous credit for his leadership, as well he should (and, just to assuage your ego, he gets correspondingly low marks in management). Bill Gates, interestingly, does not always get the same high marks, but he should as well. Unlike Steve, who leads from imagination, Bill leads from a strong fact base, typically grounded in a deep understanding of a reference competitor, one he intends to overtake and obsolete, as Microsoft did to Lotus, WordPerfect, Ashton-Tate, Aldus, Novell, Apple, and Netscape—all first-tier icons in their day. Lou Gerstner led rather than managed IBM through its historic turnaround, as John Chambers led Cisco out of the dot.com bust, and Larry Ellison led Oracle through the transition from secular to cyclical growth in enterprise IT.

Management, as we shall shortly discuss, is a necessary complement to leadership, but it does not substitute for it, as the shareholders of Apple, Dell, Charles Schwab, and Starbucks learned when these companies tried—and failed—to transition the business to a management-led model. You must lead first. That means the principles outlined above trump the implied commitments entailed by last year's operating plan. And that in turn means you need to develop a new operating plan, one that is aligned to the new core and yet still respectful of your full portfolio of obligations. No easy task, but once again, there are best practices to draw upon.

Much of the operational challenge of freeing yourself from the past consists of untangling your company from a legacy of modestly to marginally performing offers, each laying claim to just enough resource to prevent you from breaking loose.

Individually they look harmless enough, but collectively they hold you hostage, robbing your enterprise of the resources needed to serve core.

How do you cut loose from these brands? Here are a few excerpts from playbooks we have seen work for our clients, several of which we will have occasion to revisit in more detail when we get to Offer Power.

1. **Reorganize to foreground core.** Treat the investments to achieve unmatchable core as a Horizon 2 initiative on steroids, one that engages the whole company in fast-tracking it to Horizon 1 materiality in record time. In that spirit, commit to early-adopting customers for your novel capabilities, unequivocally restricting broader distribution until the initial offers are truly game changing. Put key initiatives under a single leader, and drive to a market-validated tipping point as the critical outcome. Put all functions on notice that their first priority is to support core, and incorporate into the compensation plan metrics that reinforce this message.

2. **Fund and staff your top-performing product lines 110 percent.** Give them more resources in the factory, to be sure, but more important, give them more resources in the field as well. Instead of wasting time on less-competitive offers, focus your sales force on your winners, freeing them from the distraction of an underperforming but oh-so-demanding long-tail or legacy offers. You can make 100 percent of next year's quota on the backs of your winners alone—in fact, it will be easier to make quota because you will be spending all your time on the offers the market is telling you are your best bets.

3. **Ruthlessly optimize everything else.** Long-tail offers are typically Horizon 1 hangers-on plus Horizon
2 failed attempts. They are not assets. They are li-
abilities. Manage them accordingly To be sure, each
and every one of them has champions, both inside and
outside the company, so you cannot treat them in a
cavalier way. But manage them you must, or else they
will manage you.

4. **Repurpose talent from the long tail.** Do not pun-
ish people for having worked on long-tail offers. Do
not discard their talents. Instead reassign them to the
110 percent product lines or challenge them to become
professional optimizers of legacy long tails.

5. **Recruit an outsider to break up the "web of favors."** All companies run on an internal currency of
favors, a system of IOUs that middle managers have
built up among themselves over the years, asking each
other for help on projects and providing help when
asked. These interlocking IOUs create a pervasive web
of favors that institutionalizes entitlements in every
nook and cranny of your business, locking in resources
to low-return efforts. The only way to break through
this web of favors is to install a senior executive from
outside the system who unilaterally declares an end
to the old debts and immediately starts a new web of
favors based on implementing the journey to the new
core and the long-tail rationalization needed to fund
and staff it. Much unpleasantness still ensues, but there
is plausible deniability for all the old-timers ("I tried to
get you a pass, but they wouldn't let me!"), and the organization will get through it, particularly once it sees
some success with the new initiatives.

WRAPPING UP

As you can see, at the core of creating company power is the leadership courage to make asymmetrical bets and the management prowess to execute them in tandem with running the legacy business. These bets are always multiyear and can even be a decade long in their full sweep, certainly extending well beyond the investment horizons popular with public investors. Therefore creating company power requires that the board of directors and top management be led by the CEO to take a significant risk, for often somewhere along this journey short-term performance may fall short of expectations, your stock price will take a hit, and your company could easily be put in play. You need to decide in advance whether you are willing to take the heat for staying the course; for while winning a long-term bet outperforms a short-term orientation, sacrificing for it at the outset and then abandoning it midstream produces the worst of all possible economic returns.

In the first of two case examples that follow, the CEO inherited a company that had already been disappointing investors for some time. He and his board had to decide from the very beginning, should they grow, harvest, or liquidate? They chose to grow, and over the past decade outperformed the Nasdaq by roughly 200 percent and their reference competitor by 150 percent. Here is how they did it.

Case Example: Creating Company Power at BMC—2001 to 2010

BMC provides software to manage the data centers that host computing worldwide. Historically, this has always been a products business, wherein every different vendor's hardware required specialized point products to manage. The reference competitor, then called Computer Associates, now called CA Technologies, had built a strong market position buying up aging companies, cutting back on next-generation R&D, harvesting their maintenance revenues, and leveraging a single worldwide sales force to sell a very broad portfolio of products.

BMC took a different approach, assembling a portfolio of best-of-breed offerings that competed effectively at the product level but did not roll up into suites. Although the company had some strong assets, notably in the IBM mainframe market, and was included in what the analysts called the Big Four of IT management software (the other three being IBM, HP, and CA), there was insufficient sales leverage in the model—no one ever bought two of anything—and at the beginning of the millennium, the company trailed CA significantly.

Bob Beauchamp took over the CEO role in 2001. Because BMC was not performing well financially at that time, his first priority was to "watertight the ship." That turned out to be a three-year journey, but rather than defer vision for later (as Lou Gerstner famously did when taking over at IBM), right from the outset Beauchamp also articulated an escape-velocity vision for the category and the company. BMC would apply integration innovation to the category of data center management, transforming it into something he termed Business Services Management, or BSM, something that required BMC to provide end-to-end coverage for monitoring, analyzing, and remediating IT operations across a diverse landscape of vendors and devices, including the ability to prioritize IT responses based on how seriously IT problems were harming the end-users' business operations.

This was a declaration of core. It proposed a new trajectory for the category, and it positioned BSM as a fulcrum upon which the category could pivot. It was also declared at a time when BMC was not perceived as a leader at all and frankly had only a small fraction of the software ultimately required. Indeed, this disparity was obvious enough to cause one competitor to quip, "Well, we know what the BS stands for, but we're not sure about the M." Nonetheless, despite the short-term inability to deliver anything like the long-term promise, BMC had declared its core and, at least internally, was navigating according to that North Star.

The impact of short-term watertight-the-ship reforms was to convert BMC's existing book of business into a cash-generating machine, giving the company the acquisition capital necessary to pursue its long-term vision. BMC's key departure from the norm was to forego buying up aging installed bases for their maintenance revenues and instead to acquire more-modern software assets that could contribute directly to the end-to-end architecture needed to fulfill the BSM vision. In short, M&A became a deliberate hunt for crown jewels, which came tangibly in the form of products, intangibly in the form of technology expertise and executive talent accompanying the acquisition. Because Beauchamp continued to articulate the bigger BSM vision, many of these executives stayed past their earn-outs to participate in it. At the time of this writing, the CTO, the head of sales, and the head of one of the core business units have all come to the firm originally through an acquisition.

Breakout growth, however, did not really start until the fundamental underpinnings of enterprise computing began to shift, first with the growing adoption of software as a service (SaaS) as a business model, then with the move to cloud computing as an infrastructure model. The first of these moves put heavy pressure on systems integrators like WiPro, CSC, and Infosys, who were now operating a number of data centers that they had taken over from their clients, on what one wag has called a "your mess for less" business model. They needed to get operating leverage any way they could, and one way was to run customer service applications like BMC's Remedy in a multi-tenant way, serving many clients through the same application instance, something older software packages simply could not do.

CIOs were not exempt from the need to get operating leverage either. For example, as different IT teams would need to temporarily provision a testing platform or reserve computing capacity for a major simulation, it required enormous manual intervention to provision and tear down each instance. BMC's BSM architecture allowed IT organizations to convert this process to a self-service, self-provisioning utility, saving all involved considerable grief.

And later in the decade, as the world shifted more and more compute cycles to a managed-hosting model, the companies providing these cloud computing services had to invest ever more deeply in utility-grade internal infrastructure. They needed, in effect, an ERP system for an IT services business. In this context, data center management software, far from playing a supporting role, became the killer app itself, and BSM's modern end-to-end architecture was precisely the approach that fit the bill. This is what allowed BMC to distance itself so dramatically from its reference competitor in the latter half of the decade.

Even though both of these external changes were implicit in the BSM vision, it still took significant moments of leadership to get the company fully on board. In the case of supporting SaaS, a classic Horizon 2 initiative, Beauchamp appointed a GM for the business and assigned one of his top salesmen to him on a dedicated basis. The charter was to win, no matter what it took, and Bob held regularly scheduled e-staff meetings specifically in support of this effort, at which the GM was encouraged to surface any impediment to acceleration, and the e-staff commitment was to do whatever it took to quicken the new business's pace. This was crucial to crossing the Horizon 2 chasm.

When it came to cloud computing, it was an even tougher choice, for the cloud business model actually cannibalizes the old data center model upon which the entire industry, including BMC, had been based for decades. It was critical to get the entire executive team on board with the new vision and direction, and Bob recalls a key meeting at which the head of sales, typically a champion for Horizon 1 only, said, "If we don't get onto this new trend, we'll all be toast in a few more years." When everyone around the table nodded their heads, Bob jumped on that moment to reallocate resources to cloud. But then the same head of sales pointed out he could not magically improve sales productivity for the remaining resources, and thus by reducing headcount for Horizon 1, a decision that he fully supported, the company was putting short-term performance significantly at risk. So Bob froze all hiring on the spot except for quota-carrying reps for Horizon 1 business. The company did not miss its quarterly performance targets and did get through the transition successfully.

Now, at the end of the decade, for the first time, the company has an end-to-end suite that can truly deliver on its BSM promise. It's been a long journey, one the stock market did not really twig to until the middle of the decade, and thus a very good example of the leadership fortitude and management strength necessary to execute a *lead first, manage second* strategy.

Case Example: Creating Company Power at Rackspace—2000 to 2010

Our second case example of creating company power is Rackspace, a service provider that hosts and manages computer services, primarily on behalf of small- to medium-sized businesses.

Computer-services hosting naturally gravitates toward being a commodity business. Customers want lower prices and standardized service-level agreements, and vendors want economies of scale from highly standardized, ideally fully automated, processes. Unfortunately, it rarely gets there. The IT industry changes too fast and the permutation of possible systems interfaces is too exponentially large to support any such outcome, except under the most draconian controls—e.g., the phone company or the cable company. For any nonmonopolistic franchise, this is not an option, so caught between an uncommoditizable service and an unavoidably commoditized price, what is a managed-hosting operator to do?

Well, at the outset of the managed-hosting boom, the conventional wisdom was to (1) charge a commodity price to accelerate growth and (2) restrict customer services as much as possible to preserve margins. This latter tactic was crucial, given a business model in which you might be charging $30 per month to balance against an average of $50 for a single customer support call, $100 if it went twenty minutes. Obviously, a policy of restricting customer service would create dissatisfaction, and churn would be high, but the conventional wisdom was that you could outgrow the churn rate, develop a valuable franchise, and fix the problem downstream.

This was the game that Rackspace was playing in 2000, when it became abundantly clear to all involved that it was not winning. Indeed, as the tech implosion began to unfold, the company found itself with ninety days' worth of cash in the bank, bleeding cash every month, and with no realistic prospects of raising more funds. This is the definition of a "near-death experience."

The problem, in essence, was clear to everyone: the company's fundamental product was a losing proposition—they had to reboot, and pronto. As a result, management, led by CEO Lanham Napier, decided to jettison those losing processes, almost instantaneously, in favor of committing unequivocally to an entirely new approach to creating company power.

The new approach was based on a single principle of differentiation, to provide the very best customer service in the managed-hosting industry, bar none. This was to be the new core capability. When asked to define this new standard, one tech-support rep said, "fanatical customer support," and the term stuck. Customer-support representatives, or Rackers, as they now were called, were expected to own and resolve the problem that spawned the contact on a whatever-it-takes basis. Period.

Not surprisingly, given the behavior of their new product, as soon as the company launched this program, customers loved it. More important, they voted with their dollars. Churn plummeted, and within 120 days, the company was profitable. From a base of 300 employees at the time of this reckoning, Rackspace has since grown to 3,300, with revenues approaching $1 billion. In short, there was a great outcome, which could be traced to a single declaration of core rolled out by a CEO-sponsored set of programs. So how exactly did the leaders do this?

First, they brought together the entire company for an open-book management session, pulling no punches, so everyone knew exactly where things stood. Then they declared that fanatical customer support was the new core, effective immediately. At the same time, they introduced a revamped hiring specification that sought out people who scored high on two key attributes—technical aptitude and desire to serve. They continued the open-book meetings monthly, so that people could see the impact of any changes. And they modified the tracking metrics to emphasize things that affected customer satisfaction, like how many times the phone rang before it was answered. Indeed, they ended up revamping their overall management system to center it on customer satisfaction, using the Net Promoter Score methodology as championed by Fred Reichheld, who not coincidentally joined their board of directors.

This was just the beginning. Shortly thereafter they instituted a "straitjacket" award for the most fanatical performance in customer support during the preceding period, as voted by one's peers. These awards, continued to this day, are presented at company meetings, and the ceremonies often include relatives flown in from out of town, rarely leaving a dry eye in the house. And as for those monthly open-book meetings, how could you keep those going when a company has grown an order of magnitude and operates 24/7 globally? Answer: hold them three separate times during the same day, at 10 A.M., 3 P.M., and 10 P.M., so that people worldwide can hear the same story from the same people, live, just as every one of their colleagues did.

One final element of the fanatical-customer-support play-book is worth noting: strengths-based management. When you are hired into Rackspace, you take personality tests that identify your top five strengths in a portfolio of forty. From then on, Rackspace managers are charged to build on these strengths rather than try to focus on and correct your weaknesses. The amount of positive energy this releases should not be underestimated, and in a company whose strategy for core depends on people being upbeat and alert in every moment of engagement, it is nothing less than mission critical.

Overall, the truly impressive thing about Rackspace's rise to company power is the simplicity of its approach. It really is all about fanatical customer support. By going "all in" on this vector of investment and innovation, the company had set itself apart from its competitive set and is redefining the buying criteria of the category.

CHAPTER FOUR

Market Power: Capitalizing on Markets in Transition

M arket power is simply company power specific to a particular market segment. Within the segment, you are the top dog, the big fish in your pond. Indeed, market power is always best measured in terms of a fish-to-pond ratio, where a 50 percent share of new sales into the target market segment is the entry stake and 80 percent is more likely to be the sustainable steady state. In your pea patch, you are quite simply the vendor of choice.

Thus it is that Google is the worldwide category leader in search, but not in China, where the market leader is Baidu. Facebook is the worldwide category leader in social networks, but in Spanish-speaking countries it is hi5, and in Brazil it is Orkut. In each of these market segments, the worldwide leader doesn't have a *little* less power—it has a *lot* less, as in *none to speak of*. Customers in each of these markets have built a fence around their local vendor of choice, and that has fundamentally altered the dynamics in the marketplace.

Market power of this kind *guarantees* competitive separation from your category set. When you dominate a market segment to the point that customers and partners self-organize to marginalize your competition, you have truly achieved escape velocity. And why would market segments do this? Why would they confer on your company's exceptional bargaining power, allowing you to earn margins well above the industry standard in the global market?

The primary reason is that they want and need you to give very special attention to their particular details. Global standard products go a long way toward meeting most of the specifications for any given category, but they never go all the way to meeting all the needs. That is left either to the customer or to some intermediary. This works fine for most cases, but in some segments, some of the time, the needs are high, the specifications are demanding, and the global value chain is simply not up to the task. This creates an opening for a company to develop special products and services, often augmented by a specialized value chain, and take the segment by storm. This is the reward of niche markets.

Thus Silicon Graphics and subsequently Sun workstations took the first decade or two of business from visualization-intensive segments like oil-and-gas seismic processing, computer-aided design for semiconductors, technical publications for user manuals, industrial design for consumer products, and special-effects cinema. Thus Lecroy's digital oscilloscope became the instrument of choice for nuclear physicists, HP's 12C became the calculator of choice for real estate

agents, and Tandem computers became the engine behind all
the ATM machines that retail banking could deploy.

Now, as these examples illustrate, while niche market segments may be lucrative, they are not particularly large. This
raises the question, under what circumstances does a market-
segment-focused strategy make sense, and when is the cost
not worth the candle?

There are at least eight situations in which a segment strategy is likely to pay for itself many times over:

1. **Gaining market adoption for a disruptive technology.** This is the classic crossing-the-chasm scenario,
   wherein the goal is to accelerate mainstream accep-
   tance of a disruptive next-generation technology by
   first winning over a beachhead segment, the way Lotus
   Notes won over global consulting, cellular telephony
   won over financial services, and networked attached
   storage won over high-tech engineering.

2. **Penetrating a new geography.** Regardless of how
   strong you are elsewhere around the globe, a new geography represents a new hill to climb. Just ask Google
   about its adventures in China or Nokia about its expe-
   riences in the U.S. market. Targeting an underserved
   segment, meeting its end-to-end needs all the way, is a
   great way to get market insiders pulling you in. Once
   you get a beachhead in the new geography, once you
   have a strong reference base among some constitu-
   ency, then you are positioned to grow forward. This is
   the "land and expand" strategy as played by complex-
   systems vendors.

3. **Getting out from behind the market leader.** We
   have all heard the saying, When you're not the lead

dog, the view never changes. But how do you get out from behind a number one? You need to pull into an adjacent lane to pass. Underserved market segments provide just the opportunity. When these markets finally do commit to a vendor, their spending rate dramatically outperforms the market as a whole, giving your franchise a boost. You still have work to do to overtake number one, but you are no longer breathing its exhaust.

4. **Anchoring a turnaround.** When your company is on the ropes, you need a "can't miss" market victory upon which to pivot to recovery. There is nothing like a niche market segment for solving this problem. Regardless of the size or fitness of your fish, there is always a pond in which you can make yourself the dominant species and then nurse yourself back to health. Look at how the Mac faithful kept an on-the-ropes Apple in the game during its dark years. Look at how Public Safety is keeping Motorola's network franchise viable during its tough times.

5. **Solving for the "stuck in neutral" problem.** This is somewhat like a turnaround but actually harder to execute, because you do not have the energizing impact of a "near-death experience" to galvanize the troops. Tier 2 vendors, in particular, have a tough time energizing anyone—their customers, their partners, or their employees. Everyone tends to take their existence for granted, but no one is disposed to pay a price premium for their offerings. This portends a slow but steady slide into commoditization, acquisition, and dissolution. At any point on this decay curve, however, a management team can retake control of its destiny by targeting a

niche market segment in need and becoming its favorite candidate. Win any primary, and you have delegate votes during the nominating convention. Come in middle of the pack, and you have none.

6. **Capitalizing on a great niche opportunity.** Let's not forget, there are some great niche markets out there that any company, big or small, would like to have a leadership position in, pretty much at any time: pharmaceuticals, telecommunications, investment banking, oil and gas, automotive, health care delivery, and the like. These are highly concentrated markets where a handful of companies spend a boatload of capital on next-generation facilities and tools. The barriers to entry are high, as are the barriers to exit once you get installed, so you can build high-value sustainable franchises without ever leaving the niche. Ask Cerner about health care, ask Schlumberger about oil and gas, ask Sungard about financial services.

7. **Exploiting the "granularity of growth."** As Mehrdad Baghai has taught us in his book *The Granularity of Growth*, when markets mature and commoditize, value migrates from the core offer to the secondary elements surrounding it—test and measurement instruments for food safety in China; secure, rugged mobile computers for personnel in field service and delivery; video security to prevent shoplifting in checkout lines. Profit pools migrate to those niche segments that are more than willing to pay a premium to get their particular preferences met, and thus growth, as measured by revenue and earnings as opposed to units shipped, comes more and more from microcampaigns focusing specifically on opportunities like these.

8. **Capitalizing on a market in transition.** Here an entire segment's infrastructure is being disrupted, and every company in the segment is looking for a safe haven that is compatible with the new world order. At the time of this writing, media and entertainment, risk management in financial services, call centers for consumer services, consumer advertising, and travel and hospitality are all markets in transition, all caught in a painful bind between legacy systems that are falling into disuse and next-generation systems that do not yet deliver the goods. The first whole-offer teams to arrive at their doorsteps with true end-to-end solutions to their problems will delight them so much they will want to marry them. And despite the confines of a niche market, wholesale infrastructure replacement is sufficiently lucrative that even the largest market leader should take an interest.

These are all reasons why you would want to adopt a market-power strategy. But you need to keep in mind some limiting factors, as well. Market-power development does not pay off in its first year. It does pay off reasonably well in its second year and quite handsomely in the third, as long as you have a financial runway and the patience and discipline to stay the course.

Second, market power plays a much bigger role in a complex-systems franchise than a volume-operations one. That's because the former can readily develop niche-specific whole offers through the use of custom services, can modulate price points up and down on a case-by-case basis, can build high barriers to entry and to exit, and can be cash-flow positive throughout. A volume-operations business cannot make money at low volumes, cannot readily supplement its offers with services, cannot modulate price points, and so needs much more of a winner-take-all model.

Third, while these strategies are quite good for generating tens of millions of dollars of revenue for complex-systems companies, they do not normally generate hundreds of millions. Even when you include entry into adjacent segments, it is hard to see any niche-based strategy adding up to a billion dollars. Most level out below a half billion. That's fine for a company going through its first growth spurt, and even fine for a company of several billion in size looking to supplement its portfolio, but it is subscale for the top end of the Fortune 500. There you're more likely to use market power in conjunction with company power to build a combined strategy of organic growth complemented with one or more major acquisitions.

And finally, market-power strategies require specialized talent to execute, including some key players who are not currently on your bench at all. Whenever a generalist has to recruit a specialist, there is always risk, especially when both the level you hire at and the amount of empowerment you confer on the new hire are likely to raise eyebrows elsewhere in your firm. It is critical, therefore, to get buy-in to the need for market power prior to spending this kind of personal capital.

To navigate these trade-offs, we have developed three core rules for gaining maximum returns from targeting a market segment:

1. **Big enough to matter.** When you win leading market share in the segment, say anything over 40 percent, that amount of revenue has to be material to your enterprise's total performance—ideally 10 percent or more of total revenues. So do that math. If you are a

$100 million enterprise, market segments are a great way to double your size. That was how Documentum grew from $35 million to $350 million. If you are a $1 billion enterprise, you are pushing the limits of market-segment strategy, although you would still use it to cross the chasm with a disruptive innovation, as Sybase did with its analytics database server, taking it first to Wall Street, then to the database market at large.

2. **Small enough to lead.** This is the fish-to-pond ratio part of the math exercise. If the segment is already several hundred million and you are a new entrant, this is typically a nonstarter, although you can often carve off a high-growth subsegment and focus just there. This is how RIM was able to enter the PDA market, by focusing on mobile enterprise e-mail users as virtually their sole segment.

3. **Good fit with your crown jewels.** This allows you to take the segment by storm because, in addition to bringing focus to the party, you bring some unique capability that simply blows your target customer away. Gyration, a company with miniaturized gyroscope technology that was eventually acquired by Thomson Consumer Electronics, dominated the professional presentation market for mobile mice because you could control the screen with hand gestures. It was a small market, but big enough to matter to Gyration at the time, serving as a stepping-stone for their entry into the broader market for wireless mice and gestural remote controls.

Sticking with these three rules will help you target the right kind of opportunities. After that, you have to execute on them. That leads us to a playbook for creating market power, which we call *target market initiatives*.

CREATING MARKET POWER: TARGET MARKET INITIATIVES

Target market initiatives (or TMIs, for short) are multiquarter, multiyear efforts to win dominant market share in a target market segment. They are developed around a sequence of tactics captured in a nine-point checklist (see Figure 4.1).

This list represents the table of contents for a playbook primarily targeted at complex-systems vendors, one we have been helping our clients run for over twenty years. It is anchored in the notion that market segments are word-of-

9-Point Market Strategy Framework

Key sponsor	1. Target Customer	
	2. Compelling Reason to Buy	Core problem
Complete solution		
	3. Whole Offer	Needed for whole product
Function of whole product complexity	4. Partners and Allies	
	5. Sales Strategy	Value based
	6. Pricing Strategy	
Legitimate alternatives	7. Competition	
	8. Positioning	Differentiation
Next growth segment	9. Next Target	

Figure 4.1

mouth communities that reference each other when making purchase decisions. The goal of the playbook is to orchestrate a tipping point in your target market, after which word of mouth among customers, partners, and third parties endorses both the need to adopt a new solution and also the claim that your company is the preferred source. Once that tipping point is reached, the market actually comes to you voluntarily, dramatically reducing your marketing and sales costs while increasing your bargaining power. This is a beautiful thing.

The strategy works for all eight of the scenarios previously highlighted, but it creates the greatest returns for established enterprises when applied to scenario number 8, *capitalizing on a market in transition*. Here the shift in spending happens so quickly that the anointed vendor—rarely an incumbent— seems to come out of nowhere to decimate the competition. This creates an aura of invincibility around the new offer that can carry over into other markets, even ones not adjacent to the target market, as witnessed by Apple's iPad, clearly a consumer product, having a revolutionary impact on mobile end points for enterprise IT. And so as we walk through the nine-point model, we will be using markets in transition as our anchor case.

TARGET CUSTOMER AND COMPELLING REASON TO BUY

Our journey begins by targeting a single market in transition, one segment out of many, and it is right here at the beginning, as often as not, that management teams go astray. It turns out that the concept of *market segment* is a very slippery fish. Different constituencies in your enterprise and ecosystem use the term in very different ways, the net of which is that most segment-based strategies don't achieve the focus necessary to win. Here's what's going on:

- Sales professionals use the term *market segment* in the context of defining sales coverage and sales territories. In this usage, prospects are segmented primarily by size and by location, leading to coverage assignments like global accounts, major accounts, and indirect-channel accounts, which are further subdivided geographically into regions like New York, southeastern United States, Germany, or EMEA (Europe, the Middle East, and Africa).

Such taxonomies are useful for sorting out coverage responsibilities and commission entitlements, but they have no value for TMIs. That is because they do not align with the social structures that establish word-of-mouth communication boundaries. The key to tipping-point strategies is for prospects to hear the same message from three or four different sources, all from within their own community. "Major accounts in the Southeast" does not equate to a community—it is a bounded set only in the minds of a sales team. Thus sales territories are almost always a distraction for TMI strategies. Indeed, TMI strategies frequently play havoc with sales territories.

- A second way to segment markets is by *subcategory*. This is how industry analysts like Forrester and the Gartner Group track market share. They segment the PC category into the server market, the desktop mar-

ket, the laptop market, each of which is a subcategory
of PC. Similarly, *Consumer Reports* or J.D. Powers might
segment the automobile category into luxury sedans,
economy cars, trucks, SUVs, and the like.

Shares of subcategories are highly useful metrics for cali-
brating company power, but they are not useful for market
power. Again that is because they do not align directly with
the social structure of word-of-mouth communities, the critical transmitter of market-segment leadership perception.
Just because you own a laptop or drive an SUV doesn't mean
you participate in a community of like-minded individuals.

So then how *do* communities align? In a word, socially.
Specifically, in the social structure of business-to-business
complex-systems markets, they align by industry, profession,
and geography. That is:

- Executives in the entertainment industry all know or
  know of each other, to a much greater extent than they
  know executives in the automotive industry.
- Chief financial officers typically know peers in their
  profession across many different industries, as they
  often compete for each other's jobs.
- And people who live in the geographies of England,
  Japan, and France show a strong preference to interact
  with other people who live there, and not coincidentally speak English or Japanese or French—go figure!

For a strong TMI effect, you really want all three clicking
together. U.S.-located English-speaking CFOs in the entertainment industry—now there's a tight word-of-mouth community. To be fair, you can "cheat" on this model by relaxing

one of these three dimensions—typically industry—and still create segment power, say, around sales organizations in the United States (Salesforce.com), HR professionals in the United States (PeopleSoft), global consultancies beginning with the United States and EMEA (Lotus Notes), and the like. Also, in highly concentrated industries, you can often relax the geography standard, as in pharmaceuticals, oil and gas, and aerospace and defense, all of which transcend geographical dispersal.

This kind of "flexing" of the model creates headroom for very large corporations, which really need to find a way to exercise their global reach in order to be fully competitive and to reach materiality within an acceptable time frame. By contrast, the smaller you are, the more important it is to tighten your focus, because it is this very tightening of market dimensions that keeps the bigger fish out of your pond.

Finally, there is one other dimension of the concept of market segment that can still derail your efforts before they even get started—the false notion that segments have firm and fixed boundaries. To be sure, people actually know there are no fixed boundaries in the real world, but the execution mechanics of sales-territory assignment, sales compensation programs, and lead-generation marketing all conspire to drive organizations to simplify the concept.

This would be fine, except that sales teams are inherently interested in increasing the size of their territories and will focus incessantly on opportunities at or just beyond the edges of their pea patch. This leads to way too much time, talent, and management attention getting focused on borderline cases. You end up bickering over boundaries, all the while losing precious time in capturing the really key accounts in the segment.

So to head this problem off at the outset, point out to everyone involved that while social group boundaries are inherently fuzzy at the edges, social groups do have distinct and persistent centers. The center point of any target market segment is the "perfect target customer," the *poster child* for that segment, the pure embodiment of the type of company, people, and problems that characterize that set.

So to communicate market focus, simply build a core use case around a day in the life of your poster child, then say to marketing, "Get us in touch with people like that," and to sales, "Bring me deals that look like that," and to engineering, "Create solutions for use cases like this one," and to professional services, "Get smart about how we can help customers solve this sort of problem."

All this brings us back to the number-one item on the TMI checklist: the *target customer.* In a volume-operations market, the target customer is usually one person who may or may not be buying for another person, say a spouse or child. But in a complex-systems market, there are multiple people who must approve a single purchase order, thereby turning the target customer into a hydra-headed beast. These include the budget creator (typically a line-of-business executive), the budget release monitor (typically a controller or other financial executive), the use-case sponsor (typically a department manager, to whom the use-case users report), and a specialist team that will actually take title to the purchase and support its use (typically the IT department in the industries we consult to), not to mention the ever-present purchasing department riding herd on the terms and conditions of the deal, especially price.

So who really is the target customer, specifically in a TMI, and even more specifically when targeting a market in transition? The answer is the department manager with the problem use case, backed by the financial support of the line-of-business executive to whom that department reports. Here's why.

TMIs are about addressing unsolved problems. That means there is no budget specifically allocated to the solution, because no solution has yet emerged. But there is budget being spent on remediating the problem. That budget is coming out of the line-of-business executive's P&L and is being spent by the department manager who owns the problem process. Everyone acknowledges this is an unproductive use of funds, but in the absence of a viable solution, what else can you do?

Companies in this state have a *compelling reason to buy*, as the following examples will illustrate:

- Risk managers in investment banks trading on their own accounts who cannot accurately assess the bank's total risk position.
- Print publishers watching their circulation dwindle under the pressure of digital media.
- Health care providers whose emergency rooms have become holding areas for health services to the uninsured.
- Pharmaceutical R&D executives watching the deterioration of the industry's blockbuster drug model and the escalating costs of in-house R&D.
- Licensed software package vendors watching market share shift toward software-as-a-service business models.
- Advertising agencies watching the deterioration of media buying as an overall funding vehicle for value-added services.

- Buy-side investors faced with a dearth of independent investment advice and analysis, now that these functions can no longer be subsidized by the sell side.

In every case, there is standard infrastructure in place that does not really meet the needs of the situation. The infrastructure team is not equipped to close the gap, so the performance of the department in question is deteriorating, increasing the risk that it will jeopardize the performance of the organization as a whole. The line-of-business executive is under pressure to fix this and, most important, has resources already committed to addressing the problem—just in a very inefficient way. The department manager is under pressure to come up with a better solution.

Given all this, you can see why a well targeted TMI, especially one targeted at a market in transition, has such a great chance for success. At minimum, you will definitely get a hearing, initially with the department manager, and if you pass that hurdle, then with the line-of-business executive (or vice versa—either path works). And the ask is, try us out, and if you find we are the real deal, then redirect your current spend away from Band-Aiding stopgaps and invest in a real solution instead.

That real solution is what we call the *whole offer.*

THE WHOLE OFFER AND
PARTNERS AND ALLIES

To capitalize on a market in transition, you have to be first to arrive with a true solution to the problem at hand, or what legendary marketing professor Ted Levitt and high-tech marketing pioneer Bill Davidow taught us to call the *whole prod-uct*. Subsequently we have taken to calling this the *whole offer*, as it applies just as well to service providers as to product vendors. And because this will be an end-to-end solution to a relatively complex problem, it will typically incorporate elements coming from companies other than yours, hence the pairing of whole offer with *partners and allies*.

The key tactic for swift TMI success is to make a preemptive strike—committing to something the competition either cannot or will not match—and leverage early wins to create an insurmountable lead. When that occurs, the word goes out that you are both the real deal and the safe buy, and prospects begin to give your competitors a much tougher time, often leading to the latter's sales teams to turn elsewhere in search of greener pastures.

The perfect preemptive strike is a whole offer, ready to go, that gets right to the heart of the problem. To have such a thing at the outset of your campaign, however, is quite a stretch. You're much more likely to have a decent start and an insight or two that put you slightly ahead of the pack. How do you get to a preemptive punch from there?

Two key actions are required. The first is to hire a senior executive out of the target industry who is deeply familiar with the customer's business problem and passionate about solving it. Sometimes this person can actually be an early-adopting customer for your offer, someone who is more excited about evangelizing it than staying in his or her current role. This person performs two critical functions. The first is to help you focus your whole-offer efforts precisely on the target customer's compelling reason to buy, and the second is to leverage his or her prior business relationships to connect you to the line-of-business executives for budget and project sponsorship. People in this role also help the professional-services team prioritize which elements of the customer problem to take on in which order, as well as help the product team identify potential crown jewels to differentiate your solution.

The second action you must take early in the game is to isolate and feature a crown jewel at the heart of your solution architecture, something no other competitor has. Your sales team can redefine the entire basis of the sales competition by throwing this jewel down like a gauntlet and challenging the competition to match it. Let me give a small example.

In the early 1990s, right at the outset of the client-server software era, little Lawson Software, at the time a $40 million ERP application software company from Minneapolis, had to take on Oracle, SAP, and PeopleSoft. There was no way it could go head to head with these behemoths. It had to find a smaller pond within which it could grow to a bigger fish. To do so it targeted health care institutions, particularly ones called integrated delivery networks, or IDNs, and focused on attacking the problem of health care cost reduction through better materials management. This was at the outset of the Clinton administration, when health care cost reform was very much in the air, and poor materials management was a broken mission-critical process.

Now every ERP system has a materials management module, so how was Lawson to set itself apart? Well it turns out that hospitals stage their medical inventory on a *par cart*, a mobile unit that can be wheeled from one operating theater to another and that needs to be fully stocked at all times. This led to a lot of "just in case" duplication of inventory as opposed to a more efficient "just in time" replacement strategy. However, no other industry uses a par cart approach to inventory management, so naturally no ERP system supported it.

Lawson jumped into the breach. It quickly cobbled together a demo of par cart inventory management and promised to ship a working version in its next release. It accelerated that release, creating a separate branch of development focused on integrating the par cart capability. Its customer presentation focused on par cart–based inventory management as the key to solving the materials management challenge. And it provided extra on-site project support to get its first few customers up to speed.

The preemptive strike worked. Lawson became the segment leader, getting featured treatment at health care trade shows and solicitations from big systems integrators who wanted to expand their health care offerings with materials management. Sales forces from far bigger, more established software companies simply worked around Lawson as best they could or pursued other opportunities. The company grew an order of magnitude in the space of six years and went public, all achieved on a bedrock performance in health care.

Part of Lawson's success was partner success as well. Every installation was not only an opportunity for a systems integrator to make money but also a chance to build a relationship with executives in a market in transition. Before Lawson had the inside track, partners would give the company lip service but had no real stake in its success. But once it became the segment leader, the bandwagon effect unfolded.

There is a key lesson here: before there is a viable market, do not look to partners for much help. Your unproven bet represents a substantial opportunity cost for them, and until the odds are stacked more in your favor, this is a bad bet for them to make. If at the very outset you really do need a deep partner commitment to complete your whole offer, then target a second-tier player looking for a chance to break into the top tier, and build up the size of their reward by committing to do everything you can to get them into your deals, effectively offering them a "virtual exclusive" in return for their early support.

For the most part, however, you have to rely on professional services from your own company to drive the first few projects and backfill the gaps in the nascent whole offer. This is, in effect, a Horizon 2 effort, meaning you have to adjust organization and metrics to get the support the TMI needs. But once you get past the tipping point, you can either recruit partners to handle the repeatable solution elements or monetize professional services in what has now become a Horizon 1 opportunity.

SALES STRATEGY AND PRICING STRATEGY

The sales strategy needed to exploit a market in transition is a cut above traditional solution selling. The latter qualifies a prospect based on whether or not there is budget in place and a commitment to engage. At the outset of a market in transition, there is frequently neither. Now what?

My colleagues Philip Lay and Todd Hewlin and I addressed this challenge in our March 2009 *Harvard Business Review* article entitled, "In a Downturn, Provoke Your Customers." The principles we outlined apply equally well to preempting segment leadership in a market in transition. They include the following:

- Identify a business process and underlying system that the market transition is stressing to the breaking point.

- Call attention to the severity of the consequences of not addressing this situation immediately as well as to the improbability of conventional approaches being able to solve this problem long-term.
- Propose a dramatically different approach, one that involves shifting investment priorities and budget allocation from short-term remedial efforts to a viable long-term solution.
- Win executive sponsorship for a brief, highly focused services engagement to determine the feasibility and value of the proposed new approach.
- Based on the output of that engagement, propose an end-to-end solution to be funded by budget reallocation sponsored by the business process owner.

As you can see from the bullet points above, this is a far cry from everyday solution selling. In particular, it involves calling much higher in the prospect organization than normal and bringing to bear a more deeply informed point of view than is normally practical to develop. Both these responsibilities fall on the field marketing organization, which must adopt a practice we call *referral-based marketing*.

In referral-based marketing, you do not prospect for *leads* in the traditional sense of the term. That is because in a market in transition, people do not as yet have projects funded, so there are no leads per se. Instead, you must target "plausible suspects," specifically in the thirty to forty most influential corporations in the market segment under transition. Winning projects in five to eight of these over the next four to six quarters will create the word-of-mouth tipping point you are looking for.

Within each of these targeted firms, your marketing team must identify the line-of-business executive most likely to be responsible for the broken mission-critical business process you've targeted; then your team must figure out a path of referral that can get someone in your company a meeting with that person. The meeting's stated purpose is to discuss your company's next-generation thinking about the impending problems hitting that prospective customer's industry.

Another part of marketing's job is to capture that next-generation thinking in a succinct form and to orchestrate the referral process that gets you the meeting. Sales's job is to conduct the meeting, typically by bringing a very senior executive from your company to present your views. But this is not a sales call. You are not trying to get an order. Instead, you are trying to recruit a senior executive to sponsor taking a novel approach to a troubling problem, funding the effort by redirecting current spend away from its present uses. Typically the best person to conduct this conversation is the one you have recruited out of the target segment. And the objective of this first meeting is simply to close, or to get as next to closure as possible, on a commitment to coexplore the feasibility of your proposed approach.

All in all, this is a pretty big ask of marketing, particularly if you have built an organization focused on traditional lead generation in mature, cyclical growth categories. But there is a wonderful way to increase the odds of success considerably. It harks back to when you were first testing your whole-offer concept for the end-to-end solution, months before you were ready to actually go to market with it.

At that time, your marketing team was asked to help determine how compelling was the target customer's reason to buy and how competitive was your proposed whole offer relative to the status quo. In so doing, instead of reaching out to industry analysts (who would not be focused on this issue as there is not yet a market under way), they were encouraged to reach out to the same thirty to forty companies that are now your sales targets. So in reality you already have beachhead contacts to work.

To be sure, the marketing team ended up calling much lower in the organization than you will, and they were asking much humbler questions, with the goal of getting as much customer input as possible to help shape the future wholeoffer release. But in so doing, they inevitably gathered intelligence about the specific target company, and they almost always secured an invitation to come back and present the whole offer once it was ready. As a result, getting the desired appointment is not quite as challenging as it might at first seem, as you can put on the table specific pain points that are far from randomly selected.

All of this customization comes at a price, of course, which brings us to the topic of *pricing strategy* and its role in winning share during a market transition. Solution-based pricing is inherently value based, the returns to the customer being a function of the cost reduction and risk reduction gained from meeting a highly problematic challenge head-on. This value can often be an order of magnitude greater than the direct costs of the offering, and so discounting is normally neither required nor desirable.

For example, Autodesk is currently developing the market for 3-D simulation software for the construction of buildings. Architects have used this for years, but the company is now focusing on contractors and building owners, the value proposition being to detect and head off project-delaying disconnects among the various subsystems and subcontractors that must come together to create a complex structure. In this context consider the cost of overrunning a major construction project even one day. Compare that to what you could spend on software to prevent this outcome. The gap is so great, it becomes a no-brainer to buy, provided the whole offer really does what the vendor is promising. Pricing in such a case should never be the issue.

If, on the other hand, you discover in your TMI that price has indeed become a significant issue, it usually means you are making a mistake, typically of the following sort:

1. Talking to someone who cannot reallocate budget and therefore has to squeeze money out of existing allocations, or
2. Addressing an issue that is not as compelling as you think it is, or
3. Proposing a whole offer that either is not credible or does not properly fit the problem at hand.

Discounting price is a poor response to any of these concerns. Instead, when it comes to pricing strategies for winning market power, focus your thinking on *whole-offer pricing*, meaning the end-to-end cost to the target customer all in— that is, what is paid to you and to your partners, and what is spent internally to put the complete solution in place. Make sure this total number is consistent with all of the following:

1. The budget reallocation capability of the line-of-business executive sponsor (to be compelling, the whole-offer price must be significantly less than the current remediation spend);
2. The overall value to the customer, including time to break even on the investment (because there is always competition for funds within any organization);

3. The business interests of the partners or allies who must contribute to the whole offer (you want to make sure there is enough money here for them, or else they will not come to your party); and

4. The compensation system of the sales agents responsible for selling the whole offer (so that it is worth their while to spend their time, talent, and management attention on your offer instead of on whatever else is in their bag).

Consider the example of Documentum, which led the adoption of computerized document management in the pharmaceutical industry, focusing initially on massive New Drug Approval submissions to the FDA, sometimes exceeding 500,000 pages. The target customer was the government-affairs department in each of the top forty pharmaceutical companies. But that department had no budget for the several-million-dollar expense of the total solution. So Documentum had to make its case instead to the line-of-business executives accountable for revenue from drugs under development. Its argument was simple: A patented drug averages $400 million a year in revenue (this was in 1992), or about $1 million per day. Currently it is taking your manual document-management processes anywhere from six months to a year to assemble a fully quality-checked FDA submission. That's $200 to $400 million in lost revenue. Our system, we believe, can do it in six weeks and costs $2 to $3 million. Are there any questions?

Of course, there were. But the value proposition was so compelling that pricing was rarely an issue—*as long as the budget was being sponsored by a revenue-generating entity.* When there were hiccups, invariably it was because a cost center—either the government-affairs department or the IT organization—was trying to sponsor the project without sufficient line-of-business support.

Assuming you have success in dealing with all of the above, it is important that you, too, get your fair share of the whole-offer price. This will cover a blend of product and service and maybe even a little R&D, as well. It is important to keep this mix opaque to the marketplace, because that helps establish a value-based reference point that can support relatively high margins even after the R&D work is done and the service demands have been curtailed. These high margins are part of the higher returns necessary to warrant your undertaking market development risk in the first place.

COMPETITION AND POSITIONING

One of the rewards for attacking a market in transition is that there is no entrenched competition to overcome. Instead the competitive landscape is divided into two camps. On the one hand, you have the incumbent vendors, who have established relationships with the target company but whose offerings cannot meet the challenges of the transition; and on the other hand, you have new entrants like you, who may be able to solve these next-generation problems but do not have executive relationships or domain expertise in the target market's business processes. The market is stalled because neither alternative is sufficient to move it out of stasis.

You would think the incumbents would have the advantage here, but they are actually somewhat poorly positioned. True, their relationships are long-standing, but over the years they have drifted down from the executive suite and now reside among the systems managers and technical specialists directly responsible for maintaining the systems they sell. This is not a population eager to adopt change. The pending market transition is putting both their job performance and job security under assault, and the last thing the people on this team want to do is draw attention to themselves.

New vendors like you are at least not tainted with the systemic failures that have led to the current set of broken mission-critical business processes. This is a *positioning* advantage. Moreover, because you represent a fresh point of view, the line-of-business executive on the hot seat is more than open to hearing your story. But because he or she is not a technology expert, your story has to be told, at least initially, in the business language of the problems and not in the tech nical language of the solution.

To meet this positioning challenge, it is critical that you incorporate into your team a domain expert who is fully versed in the language and processes of the target market. His or her job is to help you get the broken process clearly in view, help you understand why the installed systems cannot possibly address the challenge at hand (usually they are part of the problem), and help you craft a credible whole offer that leverages your crown jewels to solve the problem.

Having helped craft the solution, these same people are crucial to helping position it. Because they come out of the industry you are seeking to go into, they are often familiar with the incumbent solution vendors and thus able to give them their due while still pointing out their inability to address the specific challenge at hand. And because you have recruited them into your company, they are now familiar enough with your offering to explain how it is different and why it is game changing. Leveraging all these advantages, their positioning task is first to project a credible vision for a future state in which the problem is solved and then to describe a realistic path for getting there.

In sum, your positioning is anchored in:

- Your understanding of the problem,
- The crown jewels that let you approach that problem from a new angle, and
- Your appreciation for the details and complexities of changing from the current to the future state.

Note, in particular, that positioning messages in general are not about you or your products. TMI messages are all about being in service to solving a very tough problem. It is the problem, first and foremost, that binds you to the customer, and the more you have focused your communication in dialogues about the problem—as opposed to your solution—the more powerful your position will be.

NEXT TARGET CUSTOMER

The initial target customer for a TMI is a market segment in transition. Winning the segment leadership position in that market is the point of the exercise and is its own reward. But that is not the only reward.

Once you win any segment, you have elevated yourself into a privileged class, that of companies that have garnered a strong loyal base that will stick with them through thick and thin. This base will continue to support you with references and follow-on business for a long time to come. It makes a great beachhead for entering adjacent market segments. But how do you decide where to go from your first win?

A couple of rules of thumb to keep in mind are:

- It is easier to take a new solution to the same customer than it is to take the same solution to a new customer. Customer intimacy, in other words, is a stronger card to play in the market-power game than product leadership.
- It is easier to enter a new industry than a new geography. This is largely because in the same geography you can usually leverage the same set of whole-offer partners. When you enter a new geography, you are a stranger, and if you have to recruit local companies to the team, you are behind from the outset.

Both principles point to the same underlying point: business is a *relationship* sport. Yes, we will do volume-operations transactions with perfect strangers, although even then we want the reassurance of a branded product or service. But when it comes to complex systems, we are much happier dealing with people we already know. If one of these folks introduces us to a new party, well and good—that is part of the relationship dynamic, the word-of-mouth that underpins buying decisions great and small.

So the ultimate criterion for a good *next* target customer is one that already has a relationship with one of your *current* target customers. That is the way to get the best return on both your marketing and your whole-offer investments.

WRAPPING UP

That wraps up the Nine-Point Checklist playbook for creating market power, specifically when targeting a market segment in transition. It is a remarkably reliable approach to generating escape velocity, particularly for complex-systems vendors. To conclude this chapter, we want to share a case example about a company that took these lessons deeply to heart, capitalizing on a market in transition and profiting dramatically by so doing.

Case Example: A Target Market Initiative at Sybase—2007 to 2010

In the summer of 2007, John Chen, CEO of Sybase, had more or less completed his mission as a "value investor's" CEO. He had brought Sybase back from near extinction to become a $1 billion software company with highly predictable earnings and cash flow, valued at a little more than two times revenues. In short, he had done a superb job of managing the E in Sybase's P/E ratio, but he had not really changed the price premium applied to those earnings. Now, he decided, he either needed a new challenge or he had to leave.

The challenge he embraced was to transform Sybase from a value to a growth investment. At the time, the company had some "hidden" crown jewels, both in mobile computing and data analytics, but it lacked the company power to get the larger ecosystem to take it seriously. And when Chen was advised that a market-power initiative could be a path back into company power, he confessed that Sybase, by its own self-diagnosis, was well behind in this area, having the ability to create leads but not to create market power as we were defining it.

In the latter half of 2007, the company took two key preparatory steps toward changing its situation. Under the leadership of Raj Nathan, chief marketing officer (recruited out of engineering!), it revamped its marketing organization top to bottom, realigning it around six key roles: product manager, product marketing manager, field marketing manager, corporate marketing manager, industry solutions manager, and technology marketing manager. At the same time, it activated these six roles by focusing on two TMIs, one in mobile banking, the other in data analytics for data aggregators.

By the beginning of 2008, however, the crisis in the financial sector was becoming a bigger and bigger national issue, and the data analytics team refocused its efforts on Wall Street and the challenge of risk analytics in an increasingly automated, algorithmic, and opaque trading environment. The team rallied around a domain expert, Sinan Baskan, who played the role of industry solution manager, and its New York–based regional sales leader, Eric Johnson, who played the role of the entrepreneurial GM.

Over the course of 2008, the following transpired:

- A Financial Services Council was formed, including direct reports to Chen from marketing, sales, engineering, and mobile transaction services. Chaired by the head of sales, Steve Capelli, to whom Eric Johnson reported, this council ran interference for the TMI when its needs ran counter to the normal inertia of the enterprise. In particular, it reprioritized the engineering road map to release a critical programming capability well before its scheduled time, and it reorganized the field to concentrate worldwide decision authority and field-marketing support under Johnson for the target segment.
- Corporate marketing, headed by Mark Wilson, reprioritized the entire 2008 budget to privilege efforts that supported the risk analytics TMI. This included

funding a May event at the New York Stock Exchange where Alan Greenspan was interviewed onstage for an hour, discussing the risk crisis. This event by itself helped Sybase change its profile on Wall Street. The sales force was able to reignite interest in the firm and connect with the line-of-business executives in investment banks who had the power to reallocate budget to solve the burgeoning problem. To be specific, it brought the field team into contact with over one hundred chief risk officers at a time when the overwhelming bulk of Sybase's customer relationships were in the IT departments.

- The sales team meanwhile, working with the product managers and product-marketing teams at headquarters, developed a provocation-based sales strategy to complement the referrals-based marketing being done by corporate. Each salesperson role-played a dialogue with the target line-of-business executives (who were played by Sybase senior executives), all in a fishbowl environment where everyone could learn from everyone else's mistakes and successes.

- The Financial Services Council, working closely with the sales team, tracked account penetration progress at each of forty top accounts, meeting monthly to do whatever was necessary to get stalled progress unstuck.

- Finally, as noted above, the engineering team redesigned a critical piece of programming technology in order to accelerate delivery of critical whole-offer functionality, getting it to market well ahead of the prior cadence, where it was buried deep within the proverbial "next release."

The net of all these efforts was that, despite a complete meltdown in the financial sector (or perversely, perhaps because of it), the financial systems segment outgrew the rest of Sybase *eleven to one*! This boosted Sybase's company power and bought time for it to continue investing in its mobile computing initiatives, which were three to four quarters further back in the queue. Those investments came to fruition in 2009 in a number of enterprise mobility offerings, including a critical mobile application for SAP that let them deliver their business intelligence output to BlackBerries and iPhones. And that, in turn, led to an overall interest from SAP in Sybase that culminated in their merger in 2010.

So how did Chen fare with his "growth investor" company objective? During two of the toughest years in recent economic history, he took Sybase's market cap from $2.2 billion in the summer of 2007 to $3.6 billion prior to the SAP acquisition. That acquisition came in at a whopping $5.8 billion. Not bad for three years' work, especially when you consider that the valuations in the tech sector had been deeply deflated by the 2008 downturn. And if you look back to the pivot he engineered, the fulcrum for that pivot, the thing that rejuvenated Sybase's company power and positioned it for its key moves in enterprise mobility, was the market-power initiative of 2008.

CHAPTER FIVE

Offer Power: Breaking the Ties That Bind

Thus far in our discussion of escape velocity, we have imagined the pull of the past as a gravitational field holding our rocket ships prisoner to a home planet. That is how categories and competitive sets and even market ecosystems exert their claims on companies and keep them in their place. When it comes to offer power, however, it's a different story.

To achieve escape velocity, your next-generation offers, the kind that really can free your company's future from the pull of the past—the way that valued-added services have at Akamai, the way that the BSM suite did at BMC, the way that analytic servers did at Sybase—these offers must free themselves from the entanglements of a myriad of legacy commitments, a long tail of products and promises and one-off

customizations, each with its own trickle of revenue, however paltry, each nattering for some share of the sales force's
attention, however small, each tugging at the sleeve of enterprise marketing to get some murmur of the total corporate voice, however faint. This is not gravity at work. This
reminds us more of Gulliver.

You remember Gulliver, in the first of his travels, waking
up in the land of the Lilliputians, surrounded by little
people, unable to move, his giant limbs held captive by an
infinitude of tiny threadlike ropes, staked to the ground
all about his body. Thus did the six-inch-tall citizens of
that land render him powerless to move; thus does the long
tail of your legacy offer set exert its power over your next-
generation giants.

How is this possible? How can it be that the mighty is so
subordinated to the minuscule? In the world of business, it is
easy. In any given quarter, you are doing your best to meet
your revenue commitments, and not uncommonly you find
yourself a bit underpowered to do so and very much at risk of
falling short of plan. Indeed, you are much in need of a next-
generation giant that could replenish your power. But instead,
under the pressure of events and the compulsion to make the
quarter, you find yourself taking revenue from wherever you
can get it, grasping at any and all straws, fearful of cutting off
any source of funds, however small.

We call this behavior *picking up dimes in front of a steam-
roller*, and while you know as well as we do this is an unworthy occupation, frankly you do not see any alternative.
And so you fall into a pattern we call *majoring in minors*,
in which the better part of the power your enterprise can
deploy is diffused across a plethora of inconsequential

transactions, all of which may, or even worse, may not equate to making the quarter. When this tactic does succeed, you get to start the next quarter even further behind the eight ball and see if you can pull it off again. And when eventually you do miss the quarter, as inevitably you must because you have not invested in anything that would allow you to really take charge of your destiny, you get to add the ultimate insult to injury, watching a competitor come out with a next-generation product that's a far cry from what you could have done if only you had just gone and done it. That's how Sony felt when it saw the iPod and how Motorola felt when it saw the iPhone.

Life is just too short to spend this way. To diffuse power across a landscape of inconsequential transactions is to waste decades of reputation and brand building in an unworthy pursuit, and worse, to ensure that you will never achieve the escape velocity that would free you from this fate. For rest assured, it is the escape-velocity offer that you seek. Offers are the only thing in the Hierarchy of Powers that customers can actually buy. If the proof is in the pudding, they *are* the pudding. And next-generation offers is our name for that very special subset of offerings that really do change the balance of power in your marketplace.

So how are you going to break out of this tangle? Well, like Gulliver, you are going to have to innovate, not just to create your future but also to coexist in your present and to release yourself from your past. All this entails a much broader model of innovation than most people have in mind, and so it is there that we will begin.

RETURN ON INNOVATION:
PAST, PRESENT, AND FUTURE

In our study of innovation in *Dealing with Darwin*, chapter 1, we developed a model to describe three different ways in which innovation creates economic value, along with two others that actually reduce value (see Figure 5.1).

Differentiation innovation is what creates distance from competitive offers, the deepest expression of your core capabilities, the stuff that crown jewels help create, some part of which will be at the heart of your next-generation offer. This is the engine that drives your future.

Neutralization innovation is what catches you up to the changes competitors are making, what keeps you in good

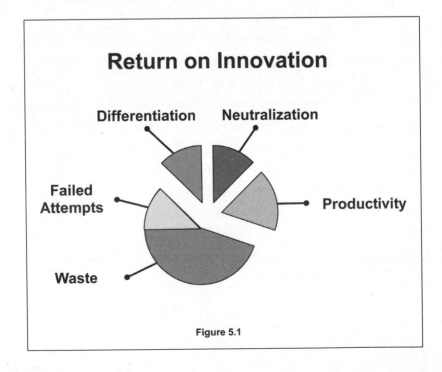

Figure 5.1

standing with your category norms, ensuring you are up-to-date with the latest improvements and compliant with the current standards. Its goal is not to make you different, but to make you the same and to do so as quickly and economically as possible. It represents the bulk of all work in the category and is the engine that drives your present.

Productivity innovation is what extricates you from your Lilliputian commitments, enabling you to resource your next-generation offers to the full extent they deserve. This is the engine that frees you from the pull of the past.

Failed attempts are just that: no program of innovation has a 100 percent success rate, or at least it shouldn't if you are really trying to push the envelope. When failures happen, you must extract all the learning you can from them and then move on.

Waste is the real killer, the bad cholesterol in your bloodstream that becomes the plaque in your arteries. It takes on different forms, depending on the return on innovation you are pursuing, something we shall dig into in detail shortly. The key thing to remember for now is that waste is recyclable as *fuel*, hidden dollars already present in your budget you can liberate on behalf of your end goals if you will only, well, stop wasting them.

Following the lead of this model, we will describe a three-part program to drive offer power in your company to escape velocity, as follows:

1. Leverage innovation in *productivity* to free your resource commitments from the pull of the past,
2. Leverage innovation in *neutralization* to meet the revenue and profit obligations of the present, and
3. Leverage innovation in *differentiation* to create suf-

ficient net new power to drive even greater future
success.

Pish posh! We should probably have time for tea as well.

PRODUCTIVITY INNOVATION: MELT YOUR DIMES INTO INGOTS

There was a time when the dimes you are picking up in front
of steamrollers were in fact dollars, and perhaps a time before
that when they were gold pieces and well worth the effort. Now,
however, each transaction entails an individually tiny but collectively lethal opportunity cost, each distracting just enough
to keep you from refocusing on dismantling the expensive infrastructure required to do this kind of business. You know you
can do better, but you never seem to find the time to do so.

Well, now's the time, and following up on the strategies we
outlined in the chapter on company power, here is specifically what you have to do:

1. Put a spotlight on the long tail of products or service
   offerings that collectively contribute, say, the last 10
   percent of your revenue stream. Banish these products from your primary distribution channel. If that
   channel is direct sales, simply make them noncom-
   missionable, not applicable to quota, not contribu-
   tive to making the 100 percent club. They can still be
   included on an order, but for no go-to-market team
   credit. If your primary channel is retail, take them off
   the prime shelf space and put them into two-tier distribution, with fulfillment orders taken over the Web.

And cease to market them whatsoever. You have not yet completely shut the valve on these things, but you have certainly blocked them from taking up valuable time and space in the go-to-market channels that matter to your overall success.

2. Put the entirety of the long tail under the governance of a single optimizing manager who is incented to extract resources and residual cash flow from these offers while minimizing customer dissatisfaction. Take revenue credit for these products away from the hosting organizations, but do not transfer the resources working on these offers. That gives them the L in a P&L without the P. At the same time, give the long-tail manager the right to take over any of these resources he or she feels will help maximize cash flow—at that point, they do transfer—but this should be entirely at the long-tail manager's discretion, because there is no way to make residual cash generation work properly if you are a safe harbor for wounded products and stranded human assets.

3. Put in place a cross-functional end-of-life (EOL) process under the governance of this same optimizing manager that proactively attacks this problem before it becomes truly pernicious. The process should give plenty of warning and visibility into the status of end-of-life offers. Salespeople, channel partners, and current customers all should get one last bite at the apple. After that, they should be redirected to the new product road map for their future needs, or to a partner if those needs cannot be met in-house.

Under this plan, business units and other P&L entities are strongly incented to integrate EOL into their core planning and operations. When they fail to do so, they get taxed by virtue of having to resource an offer for which they get no revenue credit. The company can still make money from this offer, but the BU cannot. If that does not get their attention, then perhaps a change in management is in order.

The stock-keeping unit (SKU) is the easiest measurable unit of this kind of product rationalization, but in software and services, there are special configurations, unusual terms and conditions, orphaned code branches, and the like that cause the same problems. None of these can be addressed effectively within the units that host them. Not only is the web of favors just too strong; the skill set for optimization is too weak. It is critical, therefore, to organize productivity optimization outboard of the organizations you are seeking to optimize.

Finally, be ambitious for this effort. We really do believe you can melt dimes into ingots, and that those ingots can prove to be sustainable corporate assets. There is real cash to extract here, the supply of dimes is endless, and there is always a market somewhere for them, albeit not one you will access through your mainstream go-to-market channels. Just remember, no matter what you deem to be context, no matter how lacking in value it seems to you, it can be someone else's core.

The framework that underlies the playbook for productivity innovation is the Six Levers model, modified from an earlier version presented in *Dealing with Darwin*, chapter 9. Let me recap it here so you can see how the smelter effect we are calling for is actually brought about (see Figure 5.2).

Levers 1 and 2 allow an organization to take control of a diffuse and dispersed set of products or practices by putting them under the direct supervision of a single executive, one who has a strong bent toward optimization. That executive will immediately begin to standardize disparate context activities as a

The Six Levers
Free Resources Trapped in Context Tasks

1. **Centralize.** Bring operations under a single authority to reduce overhead and create a single point of control to manage mission-critical risk.

2. **Standardize.** Reduce the variety and variability of processes delivering similar outputs to eliminate costs and minimize risks.

3. **Modularize.** Deconstruct the system into its component subsystems and standardize interfaces for future cost reductions.

4. **Optimize.** Eliminate redundant steps, automate standard sequences, streamline remaining operations, substitute lower-cost components, or otherwise cost- and resource-reduce.

5. **Instrument.** Characterize the remaining processes in terms of the variability of key parameters and develop monitor-and-control systems to manage their performance.

6. **Outsource.** Drive processes out of the enterprise entirely to further reduce overhead, variabilize costs, and minimize future investment. Incorporate vendor use of monitor-and-control systems into Service Level Agreement.

Figure 5.2

means for reducing cost and diminishing risk. This will result in a significant release of resources on a one-time basis.

Levers 3 and 4 represent a second phase of productivity improvement. Here the optimization team deconstructs the most resource-consuming processes to more precisely target the major points of greatest inefficiency or ineffectiveness. These are hived off from the rest of the standard workflow to be reengineered for substantial performance improvement. This process of isolating, hiving, and improving modules of work continues until the bulk of the available gains have been achieved.

Levers 5 and 6 represent the final phase of optimization. At this stage the optimized processes are packaged for more efficient ongoing management and administration. This may occur in some form of automated system or an outsourcing agreement. In either case, management needs instrumentation to monitor the ongoing performance of the system, and that must come before its final disposition is approved.

As you can see, the six levers represent a systematic approach to squeezing out the costs from any set of products or processes. When you centralize the long tail, expect a last-minute flurry of innovation as offers try to combine with one another to get enough bulk to survive. That is the ingot-making part of the effort. If they do not, then it is time to sluice away the detritus. In technology-based businesses, there is always something worthwhile to recycle; it just has to find a home that is more sustainable to maintain than its current orphan status.

So let's say this job is done. It won't be that easy, but you should make consistent headway if you follow this approach, and you need to attend to two other types of innovation in parallel, each of which is even more critical to your future. You have got Gulliver untied, but he is still not a free man.

NEUTRALIZATION INNOVATION: MAJOR IN MAJORS, AND QUICKLY!

How can we call something innovation when its goal is to make you the same as someone else? True innovators should be too proud to copy, shouldn't they?

Well, should Nokia have copied Apple's haptic interface, or should it have not? At the time of this writing, it has allowed Apple to retain that differentiation for three and a half years, despite the overwhelming consumer sentiment in its favor. During this time RIM copied it for their BlackBerry, and Google for its Android, and Motorola embraced the Android and Google for its Droid smart phone. As a result, all three are in the smart phone hunt in 2011, and Nokia is nowhere to be found. This has had a devastating effect on its brand, calling into question its long-term viability. Sometimes pride is misplaced.

Neutralization innovation is the energy that drives the bulk of any current book of business. It is what keeps you in good standing with your customers, your partners, your suppliers, even your competitors. It lacks the glamour of differentiation innovation, but in terms of pure ROI, risk-adjusted, it is by far the best investment you can ever make. And that is why the bulk of your people spend the bulk of their time making sure you are just keeping up with the myriad of innovations coming out of your industry.

Why is this so valuable? Think about it from your customers' point of view. Most of the time they just want to buy more of the same from the same vendors through the same channels, just so long as the offers are keeping pace with the competition. That's because the transaction costs of reevaluating a whole new raft of products, qualifying a whole new set of vendors, and adapting their current systems to a whole new set of technical and organizational interfaces is normally not worth the effort.

So while keeping pace is not a very high bar to clear, its rewards are considerable—low cost, relatively predictable sales involving knowledgeable and thus easy-to-support end users—what's not to like? How could anybody screw this up?

The answer is as simple as it is painful—people don't want to follow; they want to lead. They don't want to copy; they want to create. But now is neither the time nor place for either.

When all the market is asking for is "good enough," yet we insist nonetheless on giving more than that, and worse insist on calling this delta *value*, we are doing everyone a disservice, not least of all ourselves. Even if we present this new offer at the same old price, we have typically overengineered it for most purposes and would have done better either by reducing price to capture new, less affluent customers or by raising our gross margins to fund other initiatives within our enterprise. And worst of all, we have taken time—often lots of time—during which our offers were not competitive because we had not gotten something "good enough" out in the interim.

As we have just noted, this is the fix that Nokia got itself in relative to Apple. By contrast, look what Microsoft did to neutralize Apple's Macintosh innovations in the prior decade with its Windows operating system, or what Google is doing to Apple's iPhone innovations at present with its Android platform.

So what is the right way to play the neutralization innovation game? In a word, *speedily*. Basically, there are two primary reasons to invest in neutralization. The first is to catch up to a competitor who has achieved escape velocity with its latest offer. The goal here is not to beat them at their own game, or even to equal their success, but rather to be good enough that your customers see you as competitive. You don't dominate by these efforts—you just get yourself back in the game. So the key metric is, how fast were you able to do so?

The other reason to invest in neutralization is to contribute to your industry's overall progress, producing a handful of new features from the top of your customer base's wish list, thereby showing that you are continuing to invest in their interests. Some of these may simply involve cleaning up hygiene-factor issues, others may be genuine delighters, and all are welcomed. But there is no intent here to generate escape velocity. You don't want to escape from these customers; you want to nurture the relationship with them. So nothing terribly disruptive, just good sustaining innovation to make things a bit better, and as before, the sooner the better. Don't leave openings for your competitors to get in and disrupt these relationships.

Both of these types of innovation need to be watched over carefully, because their fundamental goals run counter to the interests and instincts of R&D teams. No engineer gets up in the morning to be "good enough." "Best in class" is more like it. But here's the thing: *Best in class is a sucker's bet!*

Customers don't pay a big premium for best-in-class offers; they pay a small increment over the mean. They do pay a big premium for *beyond class*, the unmatchable offers we will discuss in differentiation innovation. And they do impose a penalty for being *not in class*, meaning you have slipped below the expected norms of any company in the category, presumably by not neutralizing fast enough. But for everything in between *good enough* and *best in class*, the premium paid comes nowhere near covering the cost.

Best in class ends up being nothing more than the most expensive version of being in class. You spend all of your R&D budget, and you have precious little to show for it. Exhibit A for this is General Motors over the past twenty years. Exhibit B is Microsoft Office over the past ten years. Exhibit C is SAP ERP over the past ten years. Contrast these massively expensive, hugely time-consuming low-yield efforts in *neutralization innovation*—remember now, we are not dealing with escape velocity here, just business as usual—with the lights-out successes of Dell in the 1990s or HP in their PC business in the past decade or Intuit over both decades. None of these companies produced an escape-velocity offer during the period, but all have leveraged frugal, well-managed, and most of all, timely neutralization innovation to great avail.

Of course the greatest neutralization innovation performance of all time goes to Bill Gates during his leadership of Microsoft. In the course of a couple of decades he neutralized escape-velocity offers from Lotus 1-2-3, MicroPro WordStar, Ashton-Tate dBASE, Aldus Persuasion, Novell Netware, Lotus Notes, and Netscape Navigator—hijacking billions and billions of dollars of revenues right from under their very noses. At no time did he have to make the best spreadsheet or word processor or file server or e-mail client to win. He had to make ones that were good enough to be competitive, and that he did with both speed and verve.

How do you do this? How do you keep R&D focused on pursuing true value creation and keep it from chasing mechanical rabbits around a racetrack? The key is to fence in the effort so that it produces the effects you care the most about, the ones that will truly resonate with your target customer. Here is a simple framework that can help with that targeting (see Figure 5.3).

The premise of this framework is that, for almost any class of purchase, customers self-segregate into one or another of these four quadrants and then choose their offers accordingly. Take yourself for an example:

- If you are very engaged in the benefits of an offer and not sensitive to its price, then you are in the *premium* quadrant, and luxury goods and services vendors worldwide seek your acquaintance. This is how I feel about Mont Blanc ballpoint pens, particularly the Authors series.
- If, on the other hand, you long for such benefits but are price sensitive, then you are in the *performance* quadrant, and you can spend hours determining which is the best buy—good, better, or best? This is how I feel

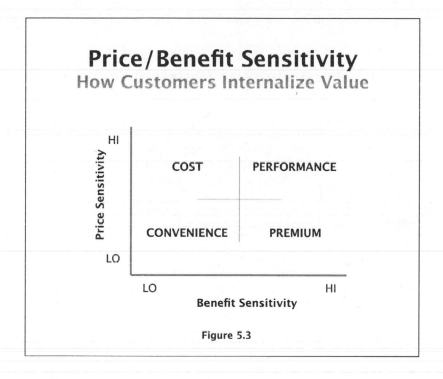

Price/Benefit Sensitivity
How Customers Internalize Value

Price Sensitivity

HI

COST   PERFORMANCE

CONVENIENCE   PREMIUM

LO

LO   HI

Benefit Sensitivity

Figure 5.3

about wine, especially Meritages; I am a bit of a sucker for a good shelf talker.

- Now, if you are not particularly benefit sensitive but you are price sensitive, then you fall into the *cost* quadrant, and lowest price is your primary decision criterion. This is how I feel about water served in restaurants—the tap water is just fine.
- And finally, if you are neither benefit sensitive nor price sensitive, then you are in the *convenience* quadrant, and you would just like someone else to make this decision for you. For me this is the zone for home-maintenance services.

Stepping back from this model, you can see, I hope, that spreading a neutralization budget evenly across all four quad-

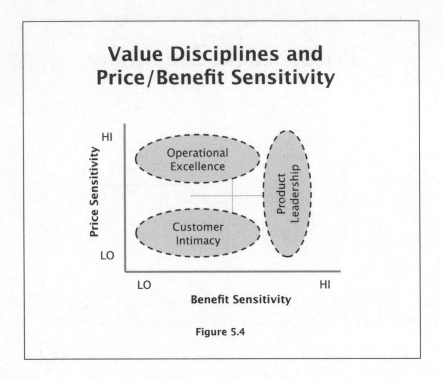

Value Disciplines and Price/Benefit Sensitivity

Figure 5.4

rants is a bad idea. Indeed, it is hard to come up with a formula that could create more waste than that one—and yet, it is the most common one we see. Why? Because when you peanut-butter innovation across all bets, then everyone gets a taste, and nobody can call you out. Unfortunately, however, you end up underperforming in the quadrants that really matter, creating openings for your competitive set.

The right way to play this model is to bet on that pair of quadrants that best aligns with your core value proposition. To keep it simple, we will use value disciplines as a proxy for whatever that may be. In that context, here are the squares on which to place your bets (see Figure 5.4).

- **Product leadership** strategies are inherently targeted at benefit-sensitive customers. It's up to you whether you want to start with premium and grow into value, or start with value and grow into premium. Just keep to the right-hand quadrants. You must neutralize every benefit that is competing for your target customers' attention.

- **Operational excellence** strategies are inherently targeted at price-sensitive customers. Whether you start with a commoditization play on the left and grow into quality, or start with quality and pare down for lowest cost, just make sure you focus your innovation budget on the upper two quadrants. You cannot allow a lower-priced offer to go unchallenged.

- **Customer intimacy** strategies, by contrast, are all about earning a price premium and thus attracting customers who are not price sensitive. Whether you are playing a premium game or a convenience game is up to you, but this is one case where the one does not normally grow into the other. You should probably stick to just one of the bottom two quadrants to get the best bang for your innovation buck. You cannot allow some other vendor to worm their way past you in your target customers' affections.

However you end up sorting out your priorities, just remember two rules: *Don't chase* and *Don't apologize*. That is, maintain the discipline of focusing your neutralization efforts away from the two quadrants that don't matter. Let your target customers' preferences be your command. Your colleagues' second guessing should come in a very distant second.

Remember, we have been talking all this time about *neutralization*, not *differentiation*. The rules we have laid out help you keep the customers you have by ensuring that the money you spend on them goes where they will most reward it. This does not, however, help you gain new customers. Or to return to the analogy with Gulliver, we have him upright and operating as a free man in Lilliput, but we still have no way to get him back home. For that we will need a stronger value proposition, one that can woo away our target customers free from their current vendor loyalties and win them over as first-time buyers. In short, what we now need is *differentiation innovation*.

DIFFERENTIATION INNOVATION: "TAKE IT TO THE LIMIT, ONE MORE TIME"

When we talk about differentiation, we have to be careful. Everything is different from everything else, so by definition

Creating the Unmatchable Offer
The Core/Context Model

	Core Unmatchable Differentiation	**Context** Neutralizing Innovations
Mission Critical	1	2
Enabling	3	4

Figure 5.5

some amount of differentiation will result from any innovation you undertake. That is not what we are talking about here. Here, to get escape velocity, to get Gulliver out of Lilliput and on to Brobdingnag, we are talking about what Andy Grove calls the *10X effect.*

The idea is simple. For a new offer to change the balance of power in any category, it needs to deliver value along some dimension that is an order of magnitude greater than the current market standard. An order of magnitude. How are you, how is anyone with a normal budget for a next-generation product, going to accomplish that?

The answer is, by making a *very* asymmetrical bet. In the language of core and context, you are going to treat every dimension of your new offer but one as context, and you are going to ruthlessly prune your investment across this universe of possible spend in order to put all your chips on one, and only one, square on the roulette table. You may not succeed, but you sure as heck are going to get noticed.

Here is the model we use to help teams come to grips with this challenge (see Figure 5.5).

Core is whatever contributes directly to the unmatchable differentiation of the offer in question. *Context* refers to all other features and properties. Clearly, the overwhelming bulk of the content of any offer is context, not core. But this is not a situation where size matters. It only takes a tiny bit of saffron to turn rice into paella, but it is all about the saffron. Same story with core. You will do whatever it takes to get the very best ingredients for core, making sacrifices wherever else you must to do so.

Nevertheless, the trade-offs between core and context are not made in a vacuum. There is another dimension to the unmatchable offer that must be taken into account—its overall performance relative to the category's current norms, norms set in part by competitors who are off touting *their* cores. In relation to meeting norms, the key distinction is between those that are *mission-critical* and those that are simply *enabling*.

A mission-critical norm is one you cannot fail to meet. Doing so will cause your offer to lose credibility in the category, leave it open to competitive attack, and detract from its more innovative features. This is what happened to the Apple Newton, for example, which was quite innovative for its time but which had a handwriting recognition capability that simply did not work. At the same time, it is crucial that work against mission-critical norms be resourced as *neutralization innovation*, along the lines we just laid out, as it is easy to be seduced by the siren call of *best in class*, especially when your context is someone else's core.

In activating the model, there is a priority of the quadrants relative to one another. In essence, you prioritize quadrant 1 (mission-critical core) over all other quadrant's goals, and after that, you will prioritize quadrant 2 (mission-critical context) over any enabling elements. If you have resources left after that, you will tilt them strongly toward quadrant 3 (enabling core). Quadrant 4 (enabling context), if at all possible, you will outsource.

Now given the enormous priority granted to mission-critical core, it is vital to choose this highly privileged dimension with care. First of all, make sure there are customers out there who would leap at the chance to get something 10X along the lines you have in mind. And second, make sure that the 10X improvement you seek is made possible, ideally uniquely possible, by your company's core capabilities and its crown jewels. This is key because it is unlikely you can ever create an order of magnitude differential acting on your own, and even if you could, it is unlikely you could keep others from copying you once you released your offer.

In sum, we need a highly desirable 10X effect enabled by our core capabilities and crown jewels. Consider, where you have seen examples of that? And just to keep you on your toes, I'm going to ban using Apple as an example, spectacular though it may be in this regard. Try the following instead:

- **Salesforce.com** created a 10X reduction in enterprise software installation and operating costs compared to the industry standards of Seibel, Oracle, PeopleSoft, and SAP. It did so by leveraging its core capabilities in hosted software architecture and the software-as-a-service business model.
- **Skype** created a 10X reduction in consumer long-distance telephony costs by offering it for free, anywhere in the world, as long as you were calling another Skype user. It did so by leveraging its crown jewel, a peer-to-peer Internet protocol that makes every subscriber's computer part of the underlying network.
- **Cisco** created a 10X improvement in the videoconferencing experience, creating what they call Tele-Presence, by leveraging their core capabilities in routing and switching over the Internet protocol.
- **Wikipedia** created a 10X improvement in the accessibility and currency of an encyclopedia, outpacing the global standard of the *Encyclopædia Britannica* in less than a decade and forcing Microsoft's Encarta out of business. It did so by leveraging its crown jewel, a collaborative governance model leveraging a cadre of generalist volunteer editors who in turn leverage a myriad specialist volunteer contributors.

- **VMWare** created a 10X reduction in the cost of data center provisioning by harnessing all the redundant capacity lying dormant in each and every computer and storage device. It did so by leveraging its hypervisor virtualization technology across a heterogeneous landscape of resources.

These are not exceptions. In the prior decade, Palm Computing created a personal digital assistant that was 10X more usable than the electronic organizers and pocket computers available at the time, leveraging its pen-based computing language called Graffiti; Dell gave us a 10X better shopping, buying, and support experience compared to IBM, Compaq, and HP, leveraging its Dell direct sales channel and build-to-order supply chain; and Motorola gave us a 10X more elegant mobile phone, the RAZR, leveraging its crown jewels in radio technology to enable a thinness previously unimaginable.

No, it is not particularly astounding that products deliver 10X effects. It is rather somewhat more astounding that we do not make them do so more often. How come? OK, to be fair, it is not *that* easy. But it is possible more often than one would think. So what holds us back? In a nutshell: *the asymmetry of risk.*

Established enterprises, unlike start-ups, have a lot to lose: brand reputation, customer loyalty, market capitalization, just to name the top three. Moreover, when they make missteps, they are natural targets for lawsuits, further adding to the risk side of the equation. And finally, from a personal career trajectory point of view, most organizations tend to reward managers with unblemished records, withholding the top jobs from leaders who have taken big falls in the past.

The consequence of all of the above is as predictable as it is disappointing. Would-be leaders hold themselves back, checked by the fear of making a truly asymmetrical bet, the risk of looking like a fool. Not always, of course. We do have role models, people like Steve Jobs, Bill Gates, Larry Page, Sergey Brin, Shai Agassi, Jeff Hawkins, John Chambers, and Jimmy Wales—and if there is anyone on this list whose name you don't recognize, by all means Google them; they will be there with page after page after page of hits, because that is what their kind of leadership and success in creating 10X effects leads to. Here's my point: You too can do this. You. You who may not even have one page of Google hits. You who may have a next-generation product budget that would not buy the fuel for an hour's flight in Sergey and Larry's private jet. You can do this. Not every time. Not without help. Not without some really good crown jewels. But look around—are you really ready to say that those things are not available to you right now? In most of the firms we work with, the ingredients for creating 10X effects are present most of the time. They have been present in IBM for the past two decades, as they have in GE, GM, Intel, Oracle, and HP.

If you work at great companies like these, companies that have shipped 10X offers in the past but not recently, you do not lack the wherewithal to do it again. What is holding everyone back is the asymmetry of risk, so that is what you must put on the table. Until the risk of not producing a 10X offer begins to approach the risk of attempting to produce such an offer, it will be hard for the organization to commit. Nokia understands this risk today in a way it did not several years ago. So does Motorola. So does Dell. So do Kodak and Xerox. It is no coincidence that all these companies are taking much more aggressive actions today than they were in their recent past. They are making 10X bets now, not just because they want to, but frankly because they have to.

So why wait? Do you really think your company is immune from the disruptive forces that have shaken these other companies to their foundations? Do you really think it is safe to hold back in these times? Use the Hierarchy of Powers to take a good look at your current risk profile and you may discover that the asymmetry you presume exists is not there at all, not because the traditional risks have diminished but because the novel ones have expanded. If that is the case, then making the 10X bet may be the safest thing you can do. And the sooner, the better.

WRAPPING UP ON OFFER POWER

Offer power takes up more of the total management conversation than any other element in the Hierarchy of Powers. This is certainly understandable, as it is the only tier in the model where revenue can be earned. But most of what goes into offer power is best managed close to the product, the channel, and the customer—not in executive boardrooms.

Where executives *can* make a difference in offer power on a daily basis is in organizing the company explicitly around the three goals of innovation that structure this chapter: *productivity*, *neutralization*, and *differentiation*. The key principle is that every initiative should have one of these three, and only one, as its defining objective. Where teams are allowed to pursue two or more, waste inevitably ensues, followed by mediocre performance in the market, loss of momentum and morale, and general decay.

That is the situation that the management team at Symbol Technologies inherited when it took the helm in 2003. It was also the situation at Adobe when Rob Tarkoff took over its enterprise systems business. How each of these organizations responded demonstrates exemplary engagement with offer power.

Case Example: Creating Offer Power at Symbol Technologies—2003 to 2006

When Bill Nuti took over as CEO of Symbol Technologies, the company was reeling internally from the effects of an accounting fraud and externally had been experiencing a steady decline in market share over the prior five years in the very categories they led—namely, bar-code scanning and rugged mobile computing. He and his key lieutenants, Todd Hewlin, head of products; Todd Abbott, head of sales; and John Bruno, head of marketing and M&A—took matters in hand in the following ways.

Following the principle that one should articulate the future before making cuts in the present, Bruno led a repositioning of the company around three key data management capabilities—Capture, Move, and Manage—creating a comprehensive architecture that leveraged crown jewels from the first two (bar-code scanning for Capture and rugged mobile computing for Move), and creating a need for Manage (a software layer, to be developed both organically and through an acquisition, to connect these edge systems to an enterprise's core IT). In effect, the team was able to put a new category in play—enterprise mobility—and carve out its part of the market—blue-collar and gray-collar workers (the former working more outdoors, the latter more indoors) as opposed to white-collar and no-collar (the former being professionals with smart phones, the latter being low-income consumers with feature phones). This enterprise mobility strategy en-

abled the company to breathe new life into its strongest markets and provided both engineering and sales with a vision to
follow.

On the product side, Todd Hewlin confronted a highly
fragmented R&D landscape in which rafts of products were
all being created independently of one another. As a result,
the company had some seventeen thousand SKUs and $100
million in excess inventory and spares for a revenue stream
of $1 billion. He and his team laid out an operating plan to
innovate in productivity, neutralization, and differentiation
on parallel paths, all governed by a road map leading to the
enterprise mobility vision, all organized around investing in
a common platform architecture to underpin the full scope of
Symbol's Capture-Move-Manage capabilities.

This road map was key to the productivity initiative. The
team was able to map every existing product and SKU to a
point in the road map at which it would be displaced by a
platform-enabled product—in effect, its end-of-life date. In
this way some twelve thousand SKUs were targeted for elimi-
nation over a two year period. The EOL program manager,
Suzanne Wenz, drove this effort on a "no surprises" basis for
the entire two years. Customers and channel partners got
ample warnings of EOL with plenty of time to make one last
"lifetime buy" before the SKU was eliminated. And marketing
and sales were both armed with the road map and the value
propositions behind the new products so they could ease customers through this transition.

Meanwhile, development was coming out with next-generation products atop the new technology platform. This enabled more resources to go into new features as opposed to
enabling infrastructure, including the ability to:

- Make the same rugged mobile computer look like a gun, a brick, or a big PDA, depending on the customer's preference;
- Make keyboards (which wear out fast) that were field replaceable;
- Extend battery life to a full shift (a very expensive engineering task, but one that had to be done only once, after which it could be applied across the entire product line);
- Ship a variety of different devices that could all use the same cradles and accessories instead each having its own proprietary requirements; and
- Provide a common software stack so that customers' applications could run on any of the devices instead of having to be written for each device separately.

Interestingly, impressive as it is, this list of features did not create escape velocity, but as neutralization initiatives they certainly got the customers' engines revving. As it turned out, the critical differentiation vector, the one that did definitively set the new Symbol product line apart from all its competition, was a 10X improvement in ruggedness—effectively taking a major customer liability off the table. For when a rugged mobile computer breaks, the business process it is enabling comes to a dead halt. This is a huge pain point for a substantial number of field sales and service organizations.

The new product survived not two hundred (the industry standard) but *two thousand* drop tests from three feet and was the first device ever certified for drops from seven feet. This major change in standard, supported by the new features, allowed one new product line called the MC-9000 to earn a whopping $240 million in its first year—by that time over one-seventh of the company's total product revenue.

Now all of this would not have happened without innovation on the go-to-market side as well. Here the company translated its system vision into a series of vertical market initiatives led by market managers who were accountable for revenue quotas for each of their respective target markets. This helped prioritize development while ensuring that field sales had valuable propositions and products to pitch.

At the same time, product managers imposed a discipline of good-better-best onto product lines that heretofore had grown like Topsy, with dozens of variants of *better*, all competing with one another, while there was little coverage for either *good* or *best*. But the former are key to recruiting entry-level channel partners, and the latter to winning major accounts, so once the new discipline was installed, Symbol's success on both fronts jumped dramatically.

On the sales side, Todd Abbott converted a product-oriented sales force, which was selling custom solutions to every single customer, into a platform-oriented solutions sales force, aligned by vertical target market. This transition, not unexpectedly, was painful, as many people and relationships had to be reoriented or replaced. In the midst of this, when customers complained about their old "tried and true" custom solutions going to end-of-life, Abbott had to hold firm and not let even the biggest customer drive any backsliding in the productivity rationalization effort. His message to his troops was simple: Sell what you have today, not only because that is better for Symbol, not only because that is better for the customer's future, but because it is the best stuff we have.

Stop wasting your time with the old stuff, picking up dimes in front of steamrollers. Stop majoring in minors.

The net outcome of all this was to drive up product revenues from $1.1 to $1.5 billion over a three-year period, leading to an acquisition by Motorola for $3.9 billion in 2006, an appreciation in market cap of 300 percent from the time the management team took over—all done within the same set of categories, all within the same set of vertical markets, hence a real testimony to offer power.

Case Example: Creating Offer Power at Adobe—2008 to 2011

In 2008 Rob Tarkoff was head of strategy and M&A for Adobe, famed earlier in its history for PostScript printing and the Acrobat Reader, touted more recently for its Creative Suite for digital designers and its Macromedia Flash Player for video on the Web. The then-new CEO, Shantanu Narayen, asked Rob to take on a different challenge—lead the enterprise software side of a corporation that was predominantly focused on consumer markets. Tarkoff inherited a mature business in Acrobat and a stalled business in software development tools for enterprise workflow. The business was definitely stuck inside the circle of his current competitive set, and no one had high expectations the situation would change, something which inevitably leads to loss of ambition, lack of discipline, and very slow cadences in development.

What did Tarkoff do? First he articulated a whole new vision for the enterprise group. They would help their business customers renovate their consumer-facing systems to bring them up to the new user experience standards being set by Google, Facebook, and the like. They called this effort Customer Engagement Management or CEM. To bring it to fruition, they would leverage Adobe's Creative Suite, the enterprise IT tools, and the company's user experience consulting group. He launched this vision, and in the next year the company conducted projects with a handful of flagship customers demonstrating the feasibility of this offering. But people both inside and outside the company were still highly skeptical that Adobe could fulfill this vision for enterprises on a scalable basis with the tools they had.

Tarkoff's next step was to lay the groundwork for an escape-velocity move. He assigned a key aide, Rob Pinkerton, to head an initiative to pick a chasm-crossing beachhead segment, one that would take the CEM initiative through the Horizon 2 gap. Pinkerton leveraged our firm to help drive this effort. Here was Tarkoff's take on that:

> *The biggest hurdle we faced in transforming an atrophying story around Adobe's Enterprise workflow solution into a birthright to lead customer experience was getting everyone in the boat rowing together. The language, frameworks, and structure of the project gave us the confidence to do this. Every conversation became fortified by the same words, concepts, drill-downs on appropriate (rather than rat-hole) topics that helped advance the strategy and define our opportunity in the market. We saw possibilities we never imagined. More important, we developed an internal cadence that energized the business in completely new ways.*

In addition, this project allowed everyone on the team from Tarkoff on down to get laser-focused on what was core to the success of the CEM initiative. Once they did, it became clear that Adobe was underpowered to deliver in some key areas. So that led Tarkoff to champion the acquisition of Day, a critical integrating platform for the CEM offer, referred to as the "hub of online interactions" for customers in their internal strategy documents. It also led him to drive for tighter integration with Omniture, an earlier acquisition that was being managed stand-alone and by so doing gave Adobe more credibility in the offices of marketers and enterprise buyers.

As these pieces came together, Tarkoff made a series of management changes under the new rallying cry of "All in!" This upped the cadence throughout his organization, throwing new leaders (including key members of the Day team) into high-energy, almost frenetic pursuit of the CEM mantle. It fundamentally changed the rules on what was allowed and encouraged within the organization and liberated the formal and informal CEM leaders to pursue new strategies for sales enablement and solution development. At the same time Shantanu Narayen, CEO, saw the potential and gave the CEM initiative a prominent position in Adobe's quarterly investor-relations communications and in internal discussions about the core growth engines at Adobe. This was a bold move indeed because Adobe was entering a market where they had no significant track record to date and were claiming they were going to revolutionize it overnight.

The market response was extraordinary. Within the first quarter of launching the new Day-powered platform, Adobe was invited into face-to-face conversations with the top executives in over fifteen Fortune 500 companies with consumer-facing businesses. For the first half of the year the pipeline swelled as these conversations became a more prominent part of the marketing and line-of-business agenda. Adobe experienced tremendous wins at major customers, and as the company looks ahead to the rest of 2011, the prospects for growth in this sector are exceptional—significantly higher than any other portion of the business—placing the company on a very fast track to the materiality targets that signify a successful passage through Horizon 2.

Such is the power of offer power.

CHAPTER SIX

Execution Power: Engineering the Escape

E verything we have discussed to date, all the various types of power we have labored to put in place, are for nought if we cannot actually execute our escape-velocity initiative. The challenge is to deploy a next-generation initiative at scale, overcoming the inertial resistance of our current go-to-market system to do so. To fully appreciate the dimensions of that challenge and address it successfully we need to:

- Model enterprise execution dynamics in general as they evolve over the life cycle of a given generation of offers from their invention to their deployment to their optimization;
- Dig specifically into the dynamics of the transition between invention and deployment at scale, with particular attention to the criticality of achieving a tipping

point and the catalytic role of programs in that regard; and

* Map these requirements to organizational development frameworks that call out the leadership attributes and organizational structures best aligned with meeting the escape-velocity challenge.

That is the agenda for this chapter.

THE DYNAMICS OF EXECUTION

To begin with, as we have been noting all along, the dynamics of business vary dramatically, depending on whether the enterprise is pursuing a complex-systems or a volume-operations business model. In each there is an arc of execution from invention to deployment to optimization, but how that arc manifests is quite different, based on which business architecture is at work.

Here is the complex-systems version of the arc of execution (see Figure 6.1).

Complex-systems businesses innovate via the execution mode of a *project*. Early-adopting customers team up with innovative systems providers and highly accomplished professional services organizations to create unprecedented responses to exceptional challenges. This is the era of flagship customers and lighthouse references. Think the Golden Gate Bridge, the Apollo project, or Woodstock.

The challenge with the project model is that it cannot be deployed at scale. So if the market for this solution is primed to take off, the sponsoring enterprises must find some way to

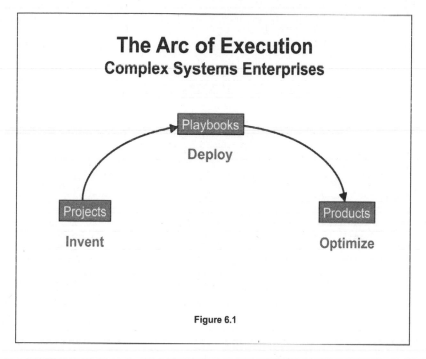

The Arc of Execution
Complex Systems Enterprises

Playbooks

Deploy

Projects

Invent

Products

Optimize

Figure 6.1

package the effort for greater reproducibility. This involves a transition in execution mode from project to *playbook*.

Playbooks are preconfigured solution kits that are tailored to specific customer requirements. Instead of working from scratch to meet uniquely bespoke project specifications, a playbook engagement is anchored on top of a pre-established architecture, one with the foundational components of the solution already in place. The deliverable is not *custom* but rather *customized*. This is what makes it reproducible at scale. Think suspension bridges, space shuttles, and a Rolling Stones tour.

As markets mature further, even more scalability is desired, along with reductions in cost and in risk. This involves transitioning the mode of execution from playbook to *product*. Here, many of the elements that had been delivered by professional services in the past are now designed to be part of the offer. The complex-systems product still requires considerable expertise to install and integrate, but the intent is to replace customization with *configuration*. Think kit houses, RVs, and home theaters.

Configurable products are the most efficient way to deliver complex-systems solutions. During the period they hold sway, they generate the highest profit margins in this execution arc. Those margins, however, can be maintained only if the systems can be continually optimized, and that optimization comes largely in the form of swapping out high-cost custom components for commodity parts and subsystems. Thus enters the volume-operations model, initially as an ally, eventually as a low-cost substitute.

Execution in volume-operations enterprises evolves through a similar arc from invention to deployment at scale to optimization, but it manifests itself in a different set of forms (see Figure 6.2).

While the product model is the optimization mode for complex systems, it is the invention mode for volume operations. This model applies equally well to physical products as it does to transaction services. In both cases, the promise is to create an efficient, functional entity that provides direct value through an immediate transaction. Think an MP3 player, an LED lighting fixture, or a health care Web site.

At their most experimental, these offers will take the form of prototypes, after which they will morph into "alpha" and "beta" releases. Then they develop into a release 1.0 (something of a sucker's bet, since what's at play is really more like a release 0.8) and eventually become releases of higher numbers and greater credibility, assuming the market adopts. Gaining that market adoption can be a real chal-

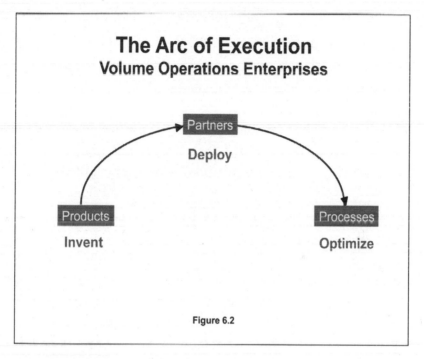

The Arc of Execution
Volume Operations Enterprises

Partners

Deploy

Products

Invent

Processes

Optimize

Figure 6.2

lenge, however, since volume-operations offerings cannot be deployed at scale without significant cooperation and investment from one or another set of potential partners. This drives a transition in execution mode from focusing on product to *partners*.

Partnerships that enable scalable deployment can take many forms, including:

- Getting physical distribution in a chain of retail outlets;
- Garnering design wins as a component or subsystem in an established complex-systems product line;
- Developing an ecosystem of partners who reinforce the purchase of the product by adding value to it;
- Wooing a set of franchisees to proliferate a proven business model;
- Securing alliances with incumbent vendors to ease the

introduction and integration of the product into their
established environments;

- Winning advertisers to monetize a no-charge media
  property or the free portion of a freemium business
  model;
- Inspiring your early customers to evangelize your
  offers, sharing them with their friends, and in effect
  behaving as a free distribution channel on your behalf.

All these are mechanisms by which volume products and
services deploy at scale. If need be, the model can power itself
alone for a while, but not forever. Sooner or later it needs a
big boost, and securing that boost is the primary focus of the
deployment phase. Think about the impact of iTunes on the
Apple iPod, or that of automobile manufacturers designing
LEDs into the front and back lights of cars, or that of advertisements from the pharmaceutical and medical products industry to support a health care Web site.

Successful deployments of a volume-operations model are
not common (according to Procter & Gamble, upward of 80 percent of new product introductions fail to get traction in the consumer package goods sector), but when they do succeed, they
stimulate an insatiable appetite for continuous improvement
in quality and cost reductions. This in turn drives a second
change in execution mode from partnerships to *processes*.

Process optimization is the hallmark capability of the volume-operations model. Inside a single enterprise, process optimization is driven by the operations team. In a distributed
network, however, things play out a bit differently. Here the
most powerful players in the network—typically, the vendors
with the really hot products or the retailers with the greatest customer reach—drive the optimization effort, extracting

more and more concessions from the less powerful players in the ecosystem, driving market expansion out and their own share of the total profit pool up. Think Microsoft, Apple, Wal-Mart, and Google, for example.

To wrap up, these are the dynamics of execution in the complex-systems and volume-operations business models, as seen from 50,000 feet. They are already part of the every-day execution management of your enterprise, and in a more granular form, they are better known to you than to me.

What may not be as obvious from your seat inside the en-terprise, on the other hand, are the organizational develop-ment principles that are optimal for each of these various modes. It is critical to get a bead on these because the kinds of leadership and the type of organization most desired vary dramatically as you move from invention to deployment to ex-ecution. Unfortunately, most companies leave the same orga-nization and the same leadership in place throughout the life cycle of a given product line, which means that for two out of three of these modes they will have a highly suboptimal team in place. This is a source of considerable underperformance in established enterprises, and it contributes mightily to the inertial resistance against letting next generation initiatives gain escape velocity.

So if we are going to truly escape, we have to find a way to keep each of these three fires—invention, deployment, and optimization—burning separately: each organized optimally for its own ends, each led by people most suited to the local mode of execution. Then we find a way to transition our of-ferings from one center to the other when the market calls for it. This is not as big an ask as it may seem. You do not have to reorganize globally to do this. But you definitely have to reorganize locally. Here's the road map to follow.

THE ART OF EXECUTION

The art of execution is based on creating local centers of excellence designed specifically to support invention, deployment, and optimization, and then investing in a fourth capability, transitioning, outboard of the other three. Here's how it all plays out.

- **The Invention Phase: Inventors and Integrated Teams.** The invention phase is typically situated in Horizon 3 at the outset, transitioning into Horizon 2 as the innovation seeks to go to market. It is a time of high investment risk but low execution risk, and the rewards go more to the visionaries than to the pragmatists. Hence the desire to put an inventor in the lead role.

Inventors are people who have a vision of the quest being undertaken and a willingness to follow their instincts to get there. They have an intuitive appreciation for what success ought to look like, even though they have not seen it yet. Think Steve Jobs and Apple's i-product line, Walt Disney and Disneyland, Mark Zuckerberg and Facebook.

The end result of invention, the product that eventually ships, must be watertight, but every step along the path to that outcome is inherently provisional. You don't really know exactly where you are going or what you are going to step in: the path to success is paved with multiple failures, each followed by quick responses, intense interrogations to learn what went wrong, and course corrections in real time.

To respond with this kind of agility requires a fully integrated team in which all the mission-critical functions—R&D, engineering, manufacturing, sales, services, and marketing—

report directly into a single entrepreneurial leader, typically a general manager. There is simply no other organizational model that can provide the low-latency responses required. There is no time to work through channels or socialize the problem to win voluntary support.

That all said, it should be clear that this model will not scale, and this is what drives the transition to the second phase in the arc of execution.

- **The Deployment Phase: Deployers and the Line-Function Organization.** The deployment phase overlaps with the invention phase for the duration of Horizon 2 and then comes into its own with the transition to Horizon 1. The focus throughout is on growth, first to reach materiality (a critical internal milestone, as we discussed in chapter 2), then to maximize market share while secular growth continues.

Deployers, the natural leaders for this phase, are competitive, performance-driven individuals who relish a challenge and love to earn top dollar for besting it. They are the ultimate pragmatists who focus intently on driving out ambiguity both from the situations they seek to master and from the metrics by which their compensation is awarded. Everything that can be quantified will be quantified and a dollar value assigned to its successful fulfillment. Hence the ginormous pay packages at Goldman Sachs, the fortunes created through stock options at Microsoft, and the extraordinary contracts paid to star professional athletes.

Deployment challenges align well with line-function organizations in which each discipline—sales, marketing, engineering, etc.—reports to a different senior executive. With ambiguity driven out of the system, members of these separate line functions can interoperate in stable predefined ways, allowing them to excel at what they do best, and allowing the workload to scale with little to no loss in effectiveness. These line functions are indeed the very same silos that we hear so much complaining about, but rest assured those complaints do not arise during the deployment phase. It is the inventors and the optimizers who are doing the screaming, the former because their inherently ambiguous world cannot be served in this way, the latter because they are offended by the exceptional inefficiency of the system. But those are not the issues on the table during a secular growth phase.

- **The Optimization Phase: Optimizers and the Hierarchical Organization.** The optimization phase overlaps with the deployment phase for the first few years after market growth transitions from secular to cyclical. This is a time of lucrative rewards for deployers whose compensation algorithms were generously set to ensure maximum efforts during the secular land grab. Now these same algorithms are substantially overgenerous, but you should not expect the deployers to tell you that. That would be up to the optimizers.

There is a serious issue at stake here. It is not just that these algorithms waste money. They hold deployer talent captive to the mature lines of business, making it very difficult to shift to the next-generation efforts. Who in their right mind would pursue a higher risk outcome that pays less than the steady-as-she-goes current system? OK, to be fair, a visionary entrepreneur probably would—but you take my point: it is as much a war to free up deployment talent to bring next-generation inventions to market as it is a cost-saving mentality that makes optimization mission critical once markets become mature.

The optimizers that lead these efforts are people who cringe at the inefficiencies in workflows and relish the opportunity to streamline or even eliminate them. They are by nature analytical, patient, thorough, and data driven. Think W. Edwards Deming and the Toyota production system, Herb Kelleher at Southwest Airlines, Ray Kroc and McDonald's Hamburger U. All delivered exceptional results by driving the nonvalue-adding elements out of the mission-critical systems under their purview.

Optimization lends itself to hierarchical structure with clear channels of authority and review. Such organizations are inherently conservative, slowing down changes to make sure they are truly for the better, guarding against unintended consequences. This allows optimization efforts to proceed like a ratchet, wringing out costs and not letting them reemerge.

TRANSITIONING TO ESCAPE VELOCITY

When you organize and staff around the life cycle of innovation, you get great traction in each of the three execution zones. Just to recap, for the complex-systems model this means great *projects* to drive entry into new categories and markets, great *playbooks* to scale up to capture market share during secular growth, and great *products* to extract maximum returns from cyclical growth. On the volume-operations side, this same arc of execution translates into great *product* R&D to enter new categories and markets, great *partner* relationships to scale out to deploy new offers during secular growth, and great *processes* to capitalize on established market positions during cyclical growth. What's not to like?

Well there is one thing not to like: *transitions*. For this zone-based approach to work properly, every successful business outcome has to be shepherded across two separate transitions. The inventor-to-deployer transition is the crossing-the-chasm challenge, the Horizon 2 gap. That, as we already know, is a bear. But the deployer-to-optimizer transition is no walk in the park either, particularly when the performance-based compensation system encourages deployers to cling to increasingly aging cash cows, as it so frequently does.

The upshot of failing to effect these two types of transition is the portfolio imbalance we highlighted in chapter 2's discussion of category power. The fact that such imbalances are pervasive should alert you to how daunting the challenge is. The solution we have been building over the course of this book is to commit the enterprise to a deeply asymmetrical allocation of resources to create breakaway capabilities, as described in chapter 3's discussion of company power. Those capabilities need to be focused on strategic tipping-point market segments in order to launch change swiftly and powerfully, as described in chapter 4's discussion of market power, and then to penetrate those segments by virtue of highly differentiated offerings, as described in chapter 5's discussion of offer power.

All well and good—provided we can drive these two types of transition to completion (see Figure 6.3).

As Figure 6.3 indicates, each transition consists of a program to drive the organization to a tipping point so that what began under one set of managers is now taken up fully by another. Transition programs, in other words, must catalyze conversions. This is not the normal way to think about pro-

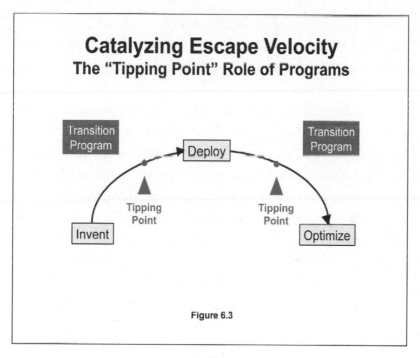

Catalyzing Escape Velocity
The "Tipping Point" Role of Programs

Transition Program

Deploy

Transition Program

Tipping Point

Tipping Point

Invent

Optimize

Figure 6.3

grams, so let us take just a minute to underscore what is required.

Most programs are level-of-effort affairs. Think training programs, or lead generation programs, or quality improvement programs. The program teams are assembled, and as long as they are working on the issue, improvement in results is expected. But when the teams stop working, those results taper off. It is a pay-as-you-go model if you will.

We're not talking about pay-as-you-go here. A transition program is a one-time intervention that changes the state of its object of focus. It is catalytic. By driving the organization to a tipping point, the center of gravity shifts, and control migrates from one locus to another: behavior changes, the culture changes, the way things get done changes, all in fundamental and nonreversible ways. In other words, this is *big* change.

Such transitions are inherently unnatural acts. To be more specific, the handoff between inventors and deployers is unnatural because visionary inventors think their work is done as soon as the first instance of the new offer has been proved to work; pragmatist deployers are not willing to take responsibility for something until there is proven market momentum behind it. This leaves the inventors fuming that no one is taking up their offers while the deployers are rolling their eyes wondering who is ever going to clue these people in.

Absent any meaningful handoff, the deployers will cling to the low-growth legacy opportunities where their bread is buttered today. This in turn creates problems for the deployer-to-optimizer transition. If the deployers won't let go, the optimizers rarely have the gumption, or frankly the clout, to take them on. Instead optimizers are more likely to retreat into passive-aggressive carping at the inefficiencies and waste. If the situation is allowed to persist, the really competent deployers will begin to defect in pursuit of better opportunities, leaving the enterprise with a hollowed out go-to-market capability that is no longer really up to the challenge of an escape-velocity initiative, and thus is even more anxious to dodge the inventor-to-deployer handoff.

This is an execution morass that many an established enterprise has found its way into. You can tell if you are there by the number of Dilbert cartoons popping up on cubicle walls. It is not an encouraging form of humor.

To break free, organizations must develop a capability to manage a fourth phase of the innovation life cycle, the act of transitioning itself. It is a phase led by people we call orchestrators, and it's something important enough to treat as a peer to invention, deployment, and optimization. Here's how this part of the life cycle plays out.

- **The Transition Phase: Orchestrators and the Cross-Functional Organization.** Orchestrators are people who excel at leading through influence, motivating others to come together to achieve some higher purpose. They are empathetic by nature and are good listeners. They always put other people first, often testing their colleagues' patience with their incessant acknowledgments of team member contributions. It is this very selflessness, however, that creates the space and energy needed to drive collaboration.

Transitions are inherently collaborations between the two types of organizations involved. The organizational model best suited to host such collaborations is the *cross-functional team*. It is made up of representatives from each of the line functions involved. The leader of the cross-functional team needs to have a clear vision of the desired future state while taking a relaxed approach about how various team members find their way to it. Members of the team must be empowered to commit their functions to the new way of going—there can be no nonrowing observers on this boat. Absent that capability to commit, cross-functional exercises degenerate into an endless series of meetings with no actionable outcomes other than to schedule the next meeting.

The purpose of this cross-functional team is to orchestrate a change in organizational state, either from invention to deployment or deployment to optimization. This change cannot be accomplished without direct sponsorship from the highest levels in the organization. Before we get to that, however, let's pause and take stock of the ground we have covered with respect to execution power and the organizational capabilities of which it is comprised (see Figure 6.4).

Four Modes of Execution

Execution Mode	Invention	Deployment	Optimization	Transitions
Type of Leader	Visionary Inventor	Pragmatic Deployer	Conservative Optimizer	Pragmatic Orchestrator
Core Competence	Creativity	Competitiveness	Control	Collaboration
Core Attribute	Spontaneous	Tough-minded	Prepared	Empathetic
Decision Style	Intuition	Experimentation	Deliberation	Consensus
Functions Most in Alignment	R&D, Creative Services	Sales, Engineering	Finance, Operations	HR, Marketing, Customer Suppt

Figure 6.4

Overall execution power (see *Living on the Fault Line*, chapter 15, for the full details behind this model) is a function of these four modes, evaluated individually and collectively. Take a moment to think about each. Where are you strongest? Where are you weakest? What does that say about your next important hire? Conversely, where might you be overweighted and need to prune?

Perhaps most important, look at the overall leader of your enterprise, whether that is yourself or someone else: what is that person's execution style? Whatever it is, it will permeate the enterprise as a whole and go a long way to setting the overall corporate culture. This will result in a strong suit in that area, but strength there will also result in a corresponding exposure in an opposite area.

The two oppositions that show up over and over again in enterprises of every shape and size are the ones between creativity and control and those between competition and collaboration. These are the four basic business cultures, each with its own go-to mode of execution, each benefitting from the balancing effects of the opposing mode. So which of these two axes better describes your enterprise?

Reflecting on these issues helps create the context for managing transition dynamics. At the end of the day, however, it is all about action. Here's how that must play out.

CATALYZING CHANGE

When looking to catalyze escape-velocity outcomes, leaders must use their power to focus change. They do this by sponsoring catalytic transition programs personally.

Catalytic programs, unlike their everyday brethren, are vehicles for leadership as opposed to management. If you try to launch a catalytic program without executive sponsorship, it signals lack of leadership, and the program will not get traction. Instead, you will have sent a message that traction is neither required nor even expected. It is all just a show. Nothing could be more demoralizing.

So while the implementers of transition programs are typically midlevel managers with superior orchestration skills, the real owners are and must be the top executives in charge. Their role is to give the program exceptional visibility, having it report out to their own staff on a monthly basis, with executives in turn reporting out on its results on a quarterly basis. We saw this in the BMC case example with Bob Beauchamp and with Lanham Napier at Rackspace. The same holds for Akamai with Paul Sagan, Sybase with John Chen, Symbol with Bill Nuti, and Adobe with Rob Tarkoff.

And we will see it again with the case examples at the end of this chapter.

Put another way, catalytic programs are the primary and most powerful levers executives have for leading large organizations. Having the final say during the annual budget process, by contrast, gives you only the appearance of power. The operating plan is actually a larger force than you are, for by the end of all the putting and taking, you are exhausted, and it is installed. That's just a fact of life, and you have to deal with it.

But catalytic programs really do give you the chance to make an impact. The inventor-to-deployer transition is the instrument by which escape-velocity outcomes are achieved. The deployer-to-optimizer transition is the mechanism by which they are funded. Being able to run the two in parallel, extracting resources from context to fund and drive core, redirecting the deployer asset to drive the next generation of growth, is the very essence of execution power.

WRAPPING UP

Execution is acting and reacting in real time to an ever-changing set of circumstances, all the while maintaining your strategic intent. Execution power, by contrast, is created in advance of the real-time moment of truth and focuses on getting the right resources in the right position for maximum impact and efficiency.

With respect to escape velocity, the critical moment of truth is passing an internal organization tipping point from promising invention to committed deployment at scale. To reach that point, top management explicitly sponsors the transition, entrusting the details to a cross-functional team led by a talented orchestrator who is accorded general-manager-like powers for the duration of the effort. Initially, the cross-functional team comprises more inventors than deployers; by the end, the team is almost all deployers.

How the deployment-at-scale journey is made depends on whether the business architecture is complex systems or volume operations. In the case of the former, the transition is from project to playbook and is essentially an internal transformation of tools and methods. In the case of the latter, it is from product to partners and is an external transformation that results in the creation or reengineering of a coordinated ecosystem, one which puts itself in service to promulgating the new offer. On the surface, these two arcs appear to have little in common, but at their core they are driven by the same force: the entrepreneurial will of the orchestrator to create a change in the state of a business.

Such things are easier to see in the concrete than in the abstract, as will be illustrated in the two case examples that follow.

Case Example: From Projects to Playbooks—Cognizant, 1998 to 2010

Even prior to the emergence of the offshore model for delivering IT services globally, custom application development and systems integration made up a vibrant and growing category, witness the successes of companies like Sapient and Cambridge Technology Partners in the 1990s. In that era, however, the business model in all cases was a *project* model in which an entire team would colocate on-site with the client. For reasons we have already noted, this model is hard to scale and virtually impossible to improve in terms of productivity, in large part because each team operates independently from every other team. A case in point: at one time HP was installing customer-relations management systems in four different divisions at the same time, leveraging the same systems integrator for all four. Much to the chagrin of all involved, there was no collaboration among any of these teams, and each installation ended up being substantially different from every other, an outcome not good for either the customer or the vendor.

When subsequently the sector shifted to assimilate an offshore model, it was not for the purposes of addressing this problem. Instead it was simply to reduce the cost of services by converting from a model of putting twenty high-cost people on-site to one of putting perhaps five such people on-site and backing them up with a much lower-cost team back in India. However, as this model scaled and new client projects were added, requiring more team members to be recruited, for the first time, all these new people were working in the same location. This created much better opportunities for knowledge sharing, and the informal beginnings of a playbook model began to emerge.

This was the world of Cognizant in 1998, a company of approximately a thousand employees doing roughly $50 million in revenue. Fast-forward to the time of this writing, 2010, and the company is doing $5 billion in revenue with over a hundred thousand employees. That is to say, it has grown not one but *two* orders of magnitude—not 10X but 100X—in little more than a decade. Clearly it had to solve the productivity and quality challenges inherent in the project model to do so. The question is, how?

It began by creating playbooks in the traditional sense,

capturing generic methodologies for application development, application maintenance, agile programming, and the
like. It hired top students from the best Indian universities
and trained them extensively in these methods. But that was
not enough. Cognizant's clients demanded specific adjust-
ments unique to their businesses. One client, for example,
had crafted a proprietary methodology for releasing code in
its environment on a weekly basis—Cognizant had to adapt
to that. Another was in the process of migrating its software
from a PC-centric to a cloud model—Cognizant had to adapt
to that as well. And the same went for a host of other clients.

Vertical market segments also drove a set of customization
requirements. When a retail client sought help installing a
merchandizing system from Oracle, it needed people who not
only understood the code but the business process as well.
The same was true for pharmaceutical companies outsourcing portions of their clinical trials workflow. In short, there
was no lack of market opportunity, but there was a limit to
how much colocation was feasible and how much informal
knowledge sharing could scale, given the exponential growth
in the workforce.

At this point, Chief Knowledge Officer Sukumar Rajagopal,
with the full support of the executive team, drove a major program investment that came to be called Cognizant 2.0. This is a
knowledge-sharing platform that combines a system of record,
wherein are stored all methodologies and artifacts from Cognizant project work worldwide, with a system of engagement,
which allows communication and collaboration throughout
the entire corporation, leveraging a number of search and
social networking technologies popularized in consumer applications like Google and Facebook. In effect, Cognizant 2.0
re-creates the experience of colocation virtually, letting indi-

vidual professionals tap into the talent and experience of their peers *without ever having to meet them in person.*

The system captures work artifacts automatically as part of the normal engagement workflow and makes them available on demand with appropriate protection of confidential information. It also provides a global personnel directory linking projects to people and vice versa, allowing someone new to a given body of knowledge to follow up with the appropriate experts. It further supports a wide-open social network where people can just shout out for help on a given subject and get both practical suggestions and advice as to whom else they should talk to.

Cognizant 2.0 was a major undertaking—at one point it involved some 750 developers—so it is not something readily copied, although Cognizant is experimenting with early-adopting clients to see how the platform might be leveraged in their businesses. But the principles it embodies can be adapted to any scale, and three in particular should be called out:

1. Work artifacts are captured online as part of normal project workflows. There is no requirement to create them offline or in someone's spare time as part of a separate knowledge-management effort.
2. People are indexed to projects and vice versa, so that individuals can follow up with each other on their own and project managers recruiting specialized talent have better visibility into who knows what.
3. The entire system is based on a *pull*, not a *push*, mechanism, so that learning happens on a just-in-time rather than a just-in-case basis.

The net of all this is that there is no shelf of binders containing a set of aging, not to say rotting, playbooks. The half-life of useful knowledge in Cognizant's business is a year or two at best, so any attempts to "capture and hold" knowledge are doomed to fail. Instead there is a kind of "catch and release" system, which looks messy at first but has proved astonishingly efficient in practice, allowing committed individuals to seek out and find what they need. In short, knowledge sharing is not a "best efforts" program at Cognizant. It is a Darwinian exercise to gain and sustain competitive separation in a fiercely competitive ecosystem that demands gains in quality and productivity every single year.

Case Example: From Products to Partners—Apple, 2001 to 2011

Unlike all the other case examples in this book, this is one where I have no inside knowledge. But the execution power Apple has demonstrated in getting from products to partners has been so spectacular that, even viewed from afar, it is a beacon for others to follow.

The story beings with the launch of what was arguably the company's first true high-volume product: the iPod. Technically, this was simply an MP3 player, but unlike all its predecessors, it was fun, it was cool, and it was amazingly easy to use. Give the boys and girls in Cupertino an A for invention.

But the real power of the iPod did not emerge until the extraordinary expansion of iTunes, with its spectacularly complete backlist supported by all four of the major music publishers. It was this act of partnering that drove the dramatic shift in deployment rates and drove Apple to the pinnacle of power it currently enjoys in the music distribution industry. How did this happen? Why did the music industry voluntarily put itself in service to Apple?

To answer this question, we have to go back to the late 1990s through the early 2000s and the rise of Napster, a free peer-to-peer file distribution network that almost overnight became a highway for transporting pirated music from one PC to another. Teenagers and college students were moving in droves to this new mode of music acquisition, and despite the illegality of this sort of file sharing, it was not clear how anyone was going to stop this emergent behavior, especially once Napster was shut down and the traffic shifted overnight to a host of comparable sites. The music industry was beside itself.

Enter Apple. Now today 99 cents per song may not seem like a lot, but in comparison to free, it is a very big deal. Steve Jobs persuaded the music moguls that at that price people would rather pay than steal, and he proved to be absolutely right. Of course, everyone had to get on the bandwagon for this to work, which they did, and all was well . . . for a while. But then it was like the "Sorcerer's Apprentice" scene in *Fantasia* where the activity of the mops and pails escalates out of control, and all of a sudden the music industry realized it had created a monster. By then, however, the genie was out of the bottle, and the world had been irrevocably transformed.

The tipping point in this journey was Jobs' negotiations with the industry: enabled by his position on Disney's board, enabled by the acquisition of Pixar, enabled by his vision about the intersection of technology and animated entertainment and his trust in John Lasseter. In other words, Jobs was enabled by an entire lifetime of commitment to these issues. That gave him the contacts and the credibility to orchestrate the partnerships that were critical to iPod's success.

You could say that was just dumb luck, except that then

Jobs went and did it again! This time it was the iPhone, and once again the designers in Cupertino created something transcendently marvelous—give them an A+ given all the copycats they have inspired. But again, a great phone in and of itself is not enough to move power permanently—as Motorola will tell you from its Razr experience. At the end of the day, volume-operations products need partners to commit to their success.

In the case of mobile phones, those partners were the carriers, and in the United States in particular, they were famous for being horrible to partner with, maintaining strict control over what are often called their walled gardens. What was Apple to do? Jobs did not have the bully pulpit to stand up like Reagan and say, "Mr. Gorbachev, tear down this wall!" He had no Joshua with a band of trumpets to take down the walls of Jericho. But what he did have was a Wi-Fi radio on the iPhone, and that proved to be the tunnel through which the sanctity of the walled gardens was breached.

Wi-Fi enabled Jobs to reach out to software developers in the same spirit that both the Macintosh and the Windows platforms had done in prior decades. By making system-development kits available to scores of these application developers and by creating the App Store through which their apps could be distributed cheaply and easily, he fostered an ecosystem that grew orders of magnitude overnight, from thousands to tens of thousands to hundreds of thousands of apps of all kinds and shapes. This was a form of partnering that the cellular industry had tried for more than a decade to pull off and failed miserably at, in large part because they were completely unwilling to open up their systems.

Now each one of those apps upped the ante on the value of an iPhone, and taken collectively, they drove the fastest adoption of any consumer device prior to that time. This meant that Apple was not dependent on carrier subsidies, which in turn ended up reversing the bargaining position. For example, now it was Verizon who had to court Apple to get in on what had been an AT&T exclusive, not the other way around.

So the iPhone displaced the iPod as the coolest consumer device on the planet, but not for long, because then along came the iPad. Who in the world would predict that lightning could strike three times in the same place, in the same decade? Once again, cool design demolished the resistance of even the most technophobic, and iPads began appearing not just in trendy spots but in boardrooms and in management meetings, in parlors and on airplanes, and it became the fastest-proliferating consumer electronic product ever, in part because it did not have to wait for an app store to evolve; it could co-opt the one already there, and the partners it entailed.

Now, however, we need to introduce a word of caution into our story. One of the most persistent attributes of market ecosystems is that they self-organize over time to curtail the further expansion of gorilla franchises. Apple is clearly the gorilla in the room, and it has been asserting itself as such of late. It banned Adobe Flash from the iPad, even though no one really wanted it to. It is driving hard terms with media properties around who owns consumers' data when they subscribe to something via the App Store. It is positioning to compete with Amazon in books and with Netflix in videos. In general, Apple is in the midst of a gigantic land grab.

This activity alienates partners. In the short term, there is little they can do about it but grind their teeth. But in the long term, partners can and will block further expansion. This is what happened to Microsoft in the 1990s, when both the cellular phone and the set-top box industries banished consideration of Windows, in large part because they did not want to be under the behemoth's thumb the way the PC industry was.

The correct response to this challenge is to engage in what we call strategic acts of generosity, where the gorilla voluntarily cedes power back to the ecosystem in return for generating another wave of goodwill. It is an idea, however, that is, as Hamlet put it, more honored in the breach than the observance. So we are not holding our breath.

That caveat aside, Apple's performance in scaling from product to partners during the past decade is a perfect case example of driving the transition from invention to deployment, and its details will be the stuff of MBA case studies for decades to come.

Conclusion

At the beginning of this book, I hoped that the idea of freeing your company's future from the pull of the past would resonate with you. Now as we reach the end, I hope it feels more directly in your grasp. To cement that feeling, let us look at one last major case example in which bringing together a number of levels of the Hierarchy of Powers created a major break from the past.

By the end of the 1980s, IBM, the single most influential company that high tech had ever seen, had lost its way. In the early 1990s, it turned in such a catastrophic performance that even its most loyal supporters questioned its reason to be and were calling for its breakup. Instead Lou Gerstner and his team were able to engineer a now-famous turnaround, restoring a commitment and then a capability to be *the end-to-end solution provider for information technology to global enterprises*. That was what they decided the world wanted IBM to be, and subsequent events have proved them right. This was their core, the foundation upon which they would restore the company's power.

In choosing this escape trajectory, they capitalized on several of IBM's crown jewels: its long-standing customer relationships anchored in the original mainframe business, its deep service capabilities, and its brand reputation for end-to-end delivery. The team took these to a new level by refocusing the company on whole new classes of offers. That is, they transformed the decaying offer power of their legacy, prioritizing service offers over products and software offers over hardware. Then they doubled down in both areas with major crown-jewel acquisitions, including PricewaterhouseCoopers in services and Lotus Notes, Tivoli, Rational, Filenet, and the like in software.

On the execution-power front, they redeployed executives from corporate-facing to field-facing jobs, letting them either sink or swim in their new customer-intimate assignments. They encouraged the services teams to support competitors' products, not just IBM's, because that is inherent in keeping an end-to-end commitment. They leveraged broad system-maintenance pricing agreements to help middle-of-the-road products compete against best-of-breed point solutions. In short, they tilted the whole company toward a services-oriented core. And everywhere they leveraged the complex-systems execution paradigm of projects-to-playbooks, eventually extracting themselves altogether from volume-operations businesses like printers (spun off to Lexmark) and PCs (sold to Lenovo).

Hitting the market in the middle of the 1990s, this dramatic repositioning caught HP and Sun off guard and set them back on their heels. This let IBM exploit a major category-power transition to Internet-enabled business-process reengineering at a time when everyone thought that was Silicon Valley's private pea patch. But what the Valley's engineers did not understand fully enough was that IBM's core was rooted in its abiding passion to help customers derive business value through technology investments, in part by sticking around long past the product sale just to make sure it paid off. The other companies in their competitive set just wanted to drop off their products and move on. That's not what a large portion of the world wanted, however, and so IBM was able to win the nod. In other words, their *services-led* offer model trumped their competitors' *product-led* approach.

Now, if an organization as unwieldy and disheartened as IBM was in the 1990s can make this journey, surely one as vibrant and lively as yours can do so as well. But that still leaves of the question of how: How do you actually get this done?

RECAPPING THE INVENTORY OF TOOLS

By my count, over the past five chapters I have presented some thirteen different models or frameworks nestled inside one or another level in the Hierarchy of Powers. That's an awful lot to absorb in the course of a relatively short book. So let's just pause here for a moment to inventory the full set of tools in our toolkit and remind ourselves what each one is for.

CATEGORY POWER

- The *Category Maturity Life Cycle* establishes growth expectations for categories in general. When executives map their portfolios onto this model, sharp disagreements often surface, but once these are resolved, the result provides a solid shared platform for making port-folio trade-off decisions.

- The *Growth/Materiality Matrix* displays a company's portfolio in relation to its two most important attri-butes—contribution to current returns and potential for future growth. Placing an offer in any one quadrant activates a clear and actionable set of priorities.

- The *Three Horizons* model identifies three distinct investment categories, each calling for a separate set of success metrics, and highlights Horizon 2 as a critical management challenge. This leads to a highly prescrip-tive playbook for organizing to meet that challenge.

COMPANY POWER

- The *Competitive Separation* model establishes the refer-ence competitors for a given company, identifies an unmatchable set of capabilities as its target opportu-nity, and calls out the innovation investments needed to make this highly asymmetrical bet. This is the single most important tool in the set for communicat-ing escape-velocity strategy to the stakeholders in your enterprise.

- The *Two Business Architectures* model, along with the notion of three tiers of competition in any market, helps winnow the universe of potential competitors to a relevant, referenceable set. This is a critical precursor to focusing competitive-separation strategy.

- *Crown Jewels* are unique assets that can create and sustain competitive separation. These are the energy sources that fuel escape-velocity trajectories.

MARKET POWER

- *The Nine-Point Market Strategy* framework is a playbook for creating market power by driving a targeted community to a tipping point, after which your company is generally endorsed as the preferred vendor. This set of plays is as fundamental to business as a good running game is to a professional football team.

OFFER POWER

- The *Return on Innovation* model brings into high relief the mutually exclusive outcomes of *differentiation, neutralization,* and *productivity.* It also draws attention to the large amount of waste in current practices and proposes how those resources can be repurposed to positive effect.
- The *Six Levers* model is a reengineering playbook for using *productivity innovations* to extract resources from context to repurpose for core. It is the fundamental mechanism by which innovation waste is recovered and recycled.
- The *Price/Benefit Sensitivity* model is a framework for prioritizing investment in *neutralization innovations,* typically stimulated by advances in competitors' offers. It focuses R&D on the values most consistent with the company's current customer base.
- The *Core/Context* model translates the company's competitive-separation strategy into the specific *differentiation innovations* required to launch the unmatchable offer. This is ground zero for escape velocity, the place where strategic intent is transformed into economic action.

EXECUTION POWER

- The *Arc of Execution* model and its companion, the *Four Modes of Execution*, provide a framework for organizational design and business transformation. Any escape-velocity initiative must anchor itself in its innovation mode, identify its scalability mode, and put in place a program to effect a rapid and lasting transition between the two.

Inventory complete. This entire body of intellectual property is devoted to the single goal of helping you to free your company's future from the pull of the past. But it still doesn't fully answer the question of how. What is the playbook for putting all these models to work?

The one we use is organized around *vision*, *strategy*, and *execution*. At any given time, one of these three typically calls out for attention more than the other two. In Stage C of the category maturity life cycle, when markets are stable and growth is cyclical, it is normally execution that needs attention. Conversely, in Stage A, when markets are being disrupted, it is a reframing of the vision that must be achieved. And finally, in Stage B, when they are undergoing secular growth change, whether positively or negatively, it is typically strategy that gets top billing.

So to close this book, we are going to outline three generic playbooks for transforming execution, vision, and strategy. It will be your job to decide which of these playbooks is most pertinent to the situation your company finds itself in currently.

TRANSFORMING EXECUTION

The underlying assumption of this playbook is that your market is mature with cyclical growth, your position long ago established, and that you are sort of stuck in neutral. Moreover, you are losing ground to competitors, not dramatically but with an increasing inevitability. Morale is declining, and prospects in general are somewhat dim. There is nothing wrong with your vision—the world does not need to be rethought. There isn't anything wrong with your strategy per se, either—it ought to work. You just aren't getting the traction you believe you should.

Time to run a set of plays around transforming execution, something along the lines of the following:

- First of all, ignore the top two levels in the Hierarchy of Powers and focus just on the bottom three. That's where your action is.
- Start with an *offer power assessment*. Often execution problems begin with a lackluster offer set, which leads to compensating behaviors that end up as bad habits.
- Use the launch of a *next-generation offer* as a platform and catalyst for transforming execution. Use the various models under offer power to focus investment on core differentiation that can achieve escape velocity.
- Use the *arc of execution* model to determine your appropriate modes for innovation and scalability, and use the four modes of execution table to guide your choice of leader for each.
- Focus *yourself* on leading a transformative program to drive the internal changes needed, recruiting a pro-

gram manager to ride herd on day-to-day issues, but engaging personally at all key junctures.

- Use the *nine-point market strategy framework* to ensure an initial in-market success. It is critical that you win early to create the positive feedback necessary to drive organizational transformation.

Obviously there is a ton of work embedded in the bulleted items above, but by now none of it should seem mysterious. The key thing for execution transformations is to move swiftly while maintaining a steady cadence. Organizations need to feel themselves changing, or else they will not transform. Your main job as transformation leader is to relentlessly reinforce the changes as they are being made, reviewing them weekly, securing commitments for the following week, charting progress all the way along, and reporting it out high and wide. "Making change visible" is the mantra for this playbook.

TRANSFORMING VISION

Transforming your company's *vision* is an exercise in getting outside yourself. Such a perspective is critical whenever the status quo is under a fundamental disruption that promises to redefine the ground of competition categorywide. Regardless of your current market status, you must prepare your company to extract itself from its current web of relationships and transform itself and its role to align with the new order.

Here your playbook might look something like this:

- Ignore the bottom two levels of the Hierarchy of Powers—they will not survive the fundamental changes that are swirling around you.
- Begin by focusing intensely on your *Horizon 2 opportunities* for transforming at least a portion of your business to stake out a market leadership position under the new order.
- In this context, seek an opportunity that ideally would exist at the convergence of three trends:
  1. An emerging demand based on new technology disrupting an old paradigm,
  2. A class of customers accessible to you who participate in this demand and are looking for a vendor to lead them through this change, and
  3. Crown jewels you have that can accelerate your ability to meet these demands as well as help protect your competitive advantage once you achieve it.
- Use the *nine-point market strategy framework* to design a target-market initiative to address the Horizon 2 opportunity.
- Use the *Three Horizons model* to design a five- to ten-year vision of the future, based on the evolving adoption of your disruptive innovation, an evolution in which the Horizon 2 opportunity you have targeted is pivotal to early developments.
- Use this vision to identify the relevant set of *reference competitors* from whom you must establish competitive separation, the beginnings of which will come from your unmatchable Horizon 2 offer.
- Build a road map across all three horizons, being careful to position your Horizon 2 offer as a trailblazer of

greater things to come. Use this road map in communications with all your stakeholders to help them visualize the future you are leading them toward.

The whole point of a transformative vision is to reorient a
universe of stakeholders in light of a disruption to their status
quo. It is an act of thought leadership, by virtue of which you
expect to win their confidence and support in leading the
way through this change. This is a particularly important
message for your employees. Their jobs, their job security,
their very livelihoods are deeply threatened by the coming
disruption, and their natural reaction will be to withdraw
from it through denial. Your job as a leader is to communicate
so vibrant a vision of the future that they are willing to let go
of what they know and make the leap to the unknown. And
then your job as a manager is to make sure that the future
you have so confidently portrayed becomes real.

TRANSFORMING STRATEGY

The classic reason to change strategy is when you are in a
winnable market with good growth opportunities but you are
not winning, or at least not winning enough. At such time,
leaders must get very clear with one another about whether
this is a case of having a good strategy and simply not executing it properly or whether the current approach is putting
too much wood behind the wrong arrows. Assuming it is the
latter, here is how you might proceed:

- Ignore the top and bottom levels of the Hierarchy of
  Powers and focus on the middle three. You're in the

right category, and we've agreed it is not an execution problem.

- Focus specifically on the *competitive dynamics* in your market, spending time on each competitor to figure out what their best differentiation strategy is likely to be. Where their capabilites are uniquely strong, take these capabilities off your list of candidates for your core. You cannot afford to be "me too" at this stage of the game.
- Use this analysis, along with an assessment of your own crown jewels, to identify a vector of *differentiating innovation* that will create core capabilites setting you definitively apart from your competitive set.
- Describe an *unmatchable offer* that would dramatically capitalize on this unique set of capabilities. Make sure it is sufficiently compelling and has broad enough appeal to warrant the strategic commitment you are about to make.
- Use the *core/context model* to highlight both the differentiation and the neutralization feature sets for this offer. Wherever possible, do whatever you can to tie up the supply of the core elements.
- Use the *nine-point market development framework* to identify the critical partners and allies you need to win with your initial launch of this strategy. Bring them into your strategy discussions early enough to ensure that they are the right partners for you and that they are on board with your plan.
- Ruthlessly apply the *six levers* model to context in general, and the long tail of existing offers in particular, to ensure that the organization as a whole focuses its best energies on the new strategy.

Strategic transformations are all about overcoming the

inertial resistance of the status quo. As such, they demand leadership first, to break the ties with the past and set the direction for the future, followed by management second, to drive the asymmetrical resource allocation and translate the ideas of strategy into the behaviors and offers of execution.

CLOSING REMARKS

We have now come full circle back to the role of frameworks and the purpose of this book. Frameworks are not machines; they are vocabulary. They do not produce strategies; they enable strategic dialogues. The final piece of the puzzle, therefore, is to incorporate them into an overall strategic planning sequence. We use the one outlined in the opening chapter of this book:

1. At the beginning of the strategic planning process, commit to reimagine your enterprise from the outside in. Specifically, ask the question, *Given the changes of the past few years, what does the world really want from us now?* What opportunities, in other words, align us best with the people in the world we most want to succeed and who most want us to succeed.
2. With this question in mind, organize your approach to the planning effort around:
    a. Articulating a compelling vision of the future that others will want to support,
    b. Setting a *strategy* consistent with that vision that positions you as the leader in the markets you want to serve, and

    c. Resourcing your execution to accomplish your highest aspirations and generate superior economic returns.

3. More specifically, use the frameworks around category power, company power, and market power to develop a common vision as to what is happening in the world and how it relates to your business.

4. Go down a level and use the frameworks around company power, market power, and offer power, to develop a strategy for sustainable competitive advantage over the companies that also seek to serve the markets you have targeted.

5. Finally, with respect to execution, go to the very base of the model and use the frameworks around market power, offer power, and execution power to construct an operating plan that dramatically skews your resource allocation such that your direct competitors either cannot or will not match your commitments.

Thus it will take three separate passes to complete the strategic plan, each drawing you closer into the present while still allowing you the perspective of a longer-term outlook. In all cases, the underlying assumption is that a common vocabulary will enable strong-willed, strong-minded individuals to fully express their differences, thereby bringing to light multiple perspectives on a given challenge. The desired outcome at the end is for these same individuals to align around a common point of view, one that will enable them to make a highly asymmetrical bet and see it through to fruition.

This is an inherently collaborative vision of management. Indeed, if I had to point to the most impactful change I have experienced in my career as a business advisor, it is the reengineering of the global economy from a universe of vertically integrated corporations run by command-and-control management systems to one of highly specialized and disaggregated enterprises interoperating collaboratively to create global value chains. In this new environment, change happens much faster than ever before because the whole no longer has any way to hold back the part. And that means that market transitions and technology disruptions are much more frequent. It also means that responses to these changes must be negotiated across a broader set of constituencies, many of which you have no command or control over. Collaboration has never been more at a premium.

In a collaborative network, the advantage goes to whoever can call the tune first, identify the relevant changes under way, find the pivotal role to play, and communicate the vision in actionable frameworks. The purpose of the frameworks in this book has been to help you achieve that advantage and free your company to participate in its rewards. At this point, all that is left is for me to wish you the very best in that endeavor, and I do.

Index

Page numbers in *italics* refer to illustrations.